A Kid in God's Tree House
A Devotional Commentary on Psalm 91

Dr. Bob Abramson

Psalm 91:14

"Because he has set his love upon Me, therefore I will deliver him; I will set him on high, because he has known My name."

A Kid in God's Tree House - A Devotional Commentary on Psalm 91

Unless otherwise specified, the following applies to all Scripture quotes. Scripture taken from the New King James Version. Copyright © 1982 by Thomas Nelson, Inc. Used by permission. All rights reserved.

Scripture quotations marked (NLT) are taken from the Holy Bible, New Living Translation, copyright © 1996, 2004, 2007. Used by permission of Tyndale House Publishers, Inc., Carol Stream, Illinois 60188. All rights reserved.

Scripture quotations marked (TLBP) OR (TLB) are taken from the Holy Bible, The Living Bible Paraphrase, copyright © 1971. Tyndale House Publishers, Inc. Carol Stream, Illinois 60188. All rights reserved.

Scripture quotations marked (NIV) are taken from the Holy Bible, New International Version®, NIV®. Copyright © 1973, 1978, 1984 by Biblica, Inc.™ Used by permission of Zondervan. All rights reserved worldwide. www.zondervan.com

Scripture quotations marked "ICB™" are taken from the International Children's Bible®. Copyright © 1986, 1988, 1999 by Thomas Nelson, Inc. Used by permission. All rights reserved.

GOD'S WORD (GWD) is a copyrighted work of God's Word to the Nations. Quotations are used by permission. Copyright 1995 by God's Word to the Nations. All rights reserved.

Message Bible (MSG) Scripture taken from The Message. Copyright © 1993, 1994, 1995, 1996, 2000, 2001, 2002. Used by permission of NavPress Publishing Group.

Cover design by Ryan Stacey

Copyright © 2013 by Robert Abramson
All Rights Reserved. No part of this publication may be reproduced without the written permission of Robert Abramson.

You may contact Dr. Abramson at Dr.Bob@mentoringministry.com or through his website: www.mentoringministry.com.

Table of Contents

INTRODUCTION	A Kid in God's Tree House	1

Part One: God is Our Refuge.
Verses 1-8

ONE	The Secret Place	5
TWO	I Will Say of the Lord	11
THREE	The Assurance of Deliverance	17
FOUR	The Wings of Refuge	33
FIVE	No Fear - Not By Night, Nor By Day	39
SIX	Stop Counting. Start Believing.	47

Part Two: He Shall Give His Angels Charge Over You.
Verses 9-13

SEVEN	Possessor of Heaven and Earth	61
EIGHT	In the Care of Angels	69
NINE	Trampled Underfoot	77

Part Three: The Divine Voice of Assurance
Verses 14-16

TEN	Your Love, His Name	87
ELEVEN	Satisfaction, Now and Forever	93
TWELVE	The Divine Voice of Assurance	101
REFLECTIONS	Psalm 91: A Gift that Keeps Giving	105
APPENDIX	Additional Scriptures and Notes *"the secret place"*	A-1

Psalm 91

"He who dwells in the secret place of the Most High Shall abide under the shadow of the Almighty. {2} I will say of the LORD, "He is my refuge and my fortress; My God, in Him I will trust." {3} Surely He shall deliver you from the snare of the fowler And from the perilous pestilence. {4} He shall cover you with His feathers, And under His wings you shall take refuge; His truth shall be your shield and buckler. {5} You shall not be afraid of the terror by night, Nor of the arrow that flies by day, {6} Nor of the pestilence that walks in darkness, Nor of the destruction that lays waste at noonday. {7} A thousand may fall at your side, And ten thousand at your right hand; But it shall not come near you. {8} Only with your eyes shall you look, And see the reward of the wicked. {9} Because you have made the LORD, who is my refuge, Even the Most High, your dwelling place, {10} No evil shall befall you, Nor shall any plague come near your dwelling; {11} For He shall give His angels charge over you, To keep you in all your ways. {12} In their hands they shall bear you up, Lest you dash your foot against a stone. {13} You shall tread upon the lion and the cobra, The young lion and the serpent you shall trample underfoot. {14} "Because he has set his love upon Me, therefore I will deliver him; I will set him on high, because he has known My name. {15} He shall call upon Me, and I will answer him; I will be with him in trouble; I will deliver him and honor him. {16} With long life I will satisfy him, And show him My salvation.""

INTRODUCTION

A Kid in God's Tree House

As I began to write this book about Psalm 91, a picture formed in my mind of a tree house that had been lovingly built by a father for his child. It was a place to get high above the child's daily world and safely abide. It was where time would be spent letting all kinds of wonderful imaginations run free. Hopes and dreams were born there. One of the best things is that the father would climb up and join in the fun. Father and child, a big dad and little kid, would spend time together in a place made just for them, where anything was possible.

In many ways, *"the secret place of the Most High"* of Psalm 91 is such a place for the child of God. It offers the delights of all our heavenly Father has created for us - His sons and daughters. It is our place of safety where we can spend time with Father God, trusting Him, as we leave the cares of the world in His hands. The door is always open, ready to welcome you, where you can hope, dream and simply be "A Kid in God's Tree House."

One of the best ways to understand *"the secret place"* is to look at it as your personal place of close, intimate fellowship with God. It is a place of communion. It is a place where you share your secrets with Him and He shares His with you. Only you and He go there. It is a place where you are so close to Him that His shadow rests over you and shelters you from the storms of life. In "The Treasury of David," Robert Horn called it the "Castle of His Mighty Defense."[1] It is where *"the Most High,"* most powerful and completely awesome God of this universe wants to "hang out" with you. It is your hiding place; and, if you desire, it will be your abiding place.

When Christ died for our sins, His atonement gave us access to this *"secret place"*…any time and anywhere. *"The secret place"* is always accessible to the child of God who seeks a close, intimate relationship with Him.

As you journey into the pages of this book, let your heart open to the possibilities *"the secret place"* holds for you. Christ offers the invitation. He paid your price of admission. As you continue through the book, allow Him to draw you into depths of a relationship with Him you have not yet experienced. I promise you it will be worth every moment, as you enter into that *"secret place of the Most High."*

Dr. Bob Abramson

---

[1] Robert Horn in The Treasury of David, Volume 2, P.95, C.H. Spurgeon, Hendricksen Publishers, Peabody.

Part One: God is Our Refuge.

Verses 1-8

ONE

The Secret Place

Psalms 91:1 (NKJV)

"He who dwells in the secret place of the Most High Shall abide under the shadow of the Almighty."

Psalms 91:1 (NLT)

"Those who live in the shelter of the Most High will find rest in the shadow of the Almighty."

"This verse speaks of the great nearness of God - a condition of God's promise, bringing special benefits to both the psalmist... and to us."[2] These words, by Mary Duncan invite us, as we begin to read Psalm 91, to sense the possibility for ourselves of experiencing the great, comforting and edifying nearness of God. In doing so, we will have the opportunity to realize the power inherent in this gift of proximity to the Lord. As we draw near to Him, we will begin to understand how staying close to God is the key. His "special benefits" are available to every child of God, who has committed to dwelling with Him in the *"secret place."*

---

[2] Mary B. M. Duncan in The Treasury of David, Volume 2, P.96, C.H. Spurgeon, Hendricksen Publishers, Peabody.

To Dwell is Not to Visit from Time to Time.
"He who dwells in the secret place…"

Think about the great nearness of God in this *"secret place."* What do the feelings of being welcome in such a place bring to you? Take this a step further. Imagine not just being a welcome visitor, but invited to *"dwell"* or live there with Him as a family member. Imagine the significance this can hold for you.

To *"dwell"* is to live comfortably, securely and peacefully in a place. It refers to a condition of habitual residence. The Hebrew word used for *"dwell"* is *"yashab."*[3] From Strong's Dictionary, I have paraphrased how I view its meanings as follows:

> *"To dwell is to be quietly, constantly remaining in a place you have chosen. This is a place that affords you the opportunity to escape the pressures and uncertainties of the world; and, where rest is the distinguishing feature."*

It is the Dwelling Place of a Special Person.
"…of the Most High"

The Hebrew words for *"Most High"* are *"elyown elyown"* which is a divine name that means, *"The supreme"* or *"uppermost."*[4] This name tells us that God is the loftiest or highest, the One above all others. The implication in this

---
[3] Strong's Number H3427.
[4] Strong's Number H5945.

name is that there is none with higher or greater authority, position or power. The prophet Isaiah spoke for the *"Most High"* when he said the following:

Isaiah 57:15

"For thus says the High and Lofty One Who inhabits eternity, whose name is Holy: "I dwell in the high and holy place, With him who has a contrite and humble spirit, To revive the spirit of the humble, And to revive the heart of the contrite ones."

Our holy God, *"the High and Lofty One,"* has assured us that He dwells on *"high"* with those who have repentant and humble spirits. As we spend time with the *"LORD"* in this *"holy place,"* we will experience revival. A distinguishing characteristic of revival is that it brings strength, renewed hope and a zeal for God. Now, that is a privileged place to be. It is clear that when we dwell *"in the secret place,"* and *"wait on the Lord,"* we can expect to have our strength renewed and our hope revived. These are great foundations for flying like the eagles, soaring with great zeal for the *"LORD."*

Isaiah 40:31

"But those who wait on the LORD Shall renew their strength; They shall mount up with wings like eagles, They shall run and not be weary, They shall walk and not faint."

It is a Dwelling Place under a Special Shadow.

"...Shall abide under the shadow of the Almighty."

From this ending portion of Psalm 91:1, we may establish two things. First, the *"secret place of the Most High"* is found under His *"shadow."* A shadow is only cast over you when you are within the boundaries the shadow defines. You cannot make your own boundaries. You have to accept the borders and limits the shadow defines for you. To be in this place is to be in close proximity, and thus, in a close relationship with God.

Second, the Scripture names Him, as not only *"the Most High,"* but then calls Him *"the Almighty."* The Hebrew word for *"Almighty"* was *"Shadday,"*[5] which simply means what it says - *"Almighty"* (all mighty). The implication is that in all things, *"the Almighty"* has all power. He cannot be contested, disregarded or opposed, with any expectation of success. Whoever tries will lose. Now, isn't that comforting, knowing you can dwell with Him in complete assurance, because there is none mightier?

The psalmist used an especially descriptive word in the latter part of Psalm 91:1. It was the word *"abide."*[6] To *"abide"* means, *"to dwell or endure."* Here is my expanded paraphrase of this meaning:

> *"To abide is to continually and comfortably lodge in a place, to spend time there, to be*

---

[5] Strong's Number H7706.
[6] Strong's Number H3885 - *"luwn."*

comfortably at home... to continue in a particular attitude or relationship."

The significance of the passage becomes clear. Here is my paraphrase of Psalm 91:1. Consider how it speaks to your heart and what it can mean for you:

"Those who quietly and constantly remain at rest in that hidden place in God, will be comfortably at home, secure in their own relationship with the One who is above all others, and has the power to guarantee security, safety and peace."

Meditate on my paraphrase. Then, look to Psalm 46. You will find its message to be one of many additional Scriptures that reinforce what the Holy Spirit has said in this opening verse of Psalm 91. There is so much more that He will say to you, as you go through the remaining verses of Psalm 91. Now, let's consider how Psalm 46 agrees with Psalm 91:1.

Psalms 46:1-3, 7, 10-11

"God is our refuge and strength, A very present help in trouble. {2} Therefore we will not fear, Even though the earth be removed, And though the mountains be carried into the midst of the sea; {3} Though its waters roar and be troubled, Though the mountains shake with its swelling. Selah... {7} The LORD of hosts is with us; The God of Jacob is our refuge. Selah... {10} Be still, and know that I am God; I will be exalted among the nations, I will be exalted in the earth! {11}

The LORD of hosts is with us; The God of Jacob is our refuge. Selah"

As you conclude this first chapter, notice that three times in Psalm 46, the word *"Selah"* appears. *"Selah"* was not meant to be spoken or sung aloud. It signaled that we should stop and silently reflect on what the psalmist said, before going any further. Look once more at Psalm 91:1 and think about what this first chapter has unfolded to you. Then, let's move to the next chapter.

TWO

I Will Say of the Lord

Psalms 91:2 (NKJV)

"I will say of the LORD, "He is my refuge and my fortress; My God, in Him I will trust."

Psalms 91:2 (NLT)

"This I declare of the LORD: He alone is my refuge, my place of safety; he is my God, and I am trusting him."

The Hebrew word for *"say"* or *"declare"* used in Verse 2 is *"amar."*[7] Among its meanings, are *"boast"* and *"certify."* In times of uncertainty and even fear, I have found my immediate and best remedy is to declare aloud, or to *"boast"* of and *"certify"* my faith in *"the LORD."* I can do this with authority because of my previous experiences. I have often said that you can argue with someone successfully about many things, but never with their own experiences.

In Verse 2, the psalmist made his declaration of faith in the face of his own uncertainties and fears. The key, therefore, is to speak words of faith to yourself, to whoever else will

---

[7] Strong's Number H559.

listen and most importantly, to *"the LORD."* When the psalmist wrote, *"I will say of the LORD..."* or, *"This I declare of the LORD..."* he was also saying, *"I will say 'to' the LORD..."* or *"I will declare 'to' the LORD..."* God is listening to every word you speak. What you say ought to be an affirmation of who God is and what He constantly provides for you.

In Verse 2, the psalmist made his faith declaration that God was the only one to whom he could turn. Only He could be the psalmist's fully dependable place of safety in the face of his fears. Do not overlook the particulars of this statement. The psalmist did not say that God provided him with a refuge and fortress. He said that God was his refuge and fortress. Psalm 46:1 said essentially the same thing, describing *"the LORD"* as *"my refuge and strength..."* The psalmist's trust was in his intimate, personal relationship with God. You and I can have the same trust, without fear, doubt or wavering. He is forever faithful. It has been said, *"Loving faith on man's part shall be met by faithful love on God's part."*[8]

Throughout Psalm 91, the Hebrew word translated *"LORD"* is *"Yehovah."*[9] It means *"Self-Existent or Eternal."* He was, is, and always will be the Creator of all things, in complete control of His creation. He is the divine Person who invites us into His *"secret place,"* and who casts His protective shadow over us when we enter. Knowing this allows us to

---

[8] Taken from "The Psalms, with Notes by W. Kay." 1864.
[9] Strong's Number H3068

abide under His shadow with confidence that we will be safe from the storms of life that inevitably come.

Trust In God Determines Your Destiny.

Verse 2b (NKJV)

"My God, in Him I will trust."

Verse 2b (NLT)

"...he is my God, and I am trusting him."

Life is a constant stream of events and encounters. Some are within your abilities to manage, while others are totally out of your control. In every case, the choices you make concerning in whom you will trust determine the outcomes of your situations, and may even change your destiny. You will inevitably trust in something or somebody to validate and secure these choices.

You may choose to trust in one, or any combination of the following available options:
- Your instincts
- Your philosophies of life
- Your experiences
- Luck
- Your abilities to reason and think
- Relationships with people and their advice

Are there additional options you may find yourself choosing that might one day be found ineffective and untrustworthy? As you process your life's decisions, could they let you down? Might any or all of them be worthless, useless, and completely powerless, when you most need help?

If your trust is misplaced, you may find yourself naked of any defense, covering or security. This will open the door to fear, uncertainty, confusion, indecision, or countless other unsettling feelings. Before these unsettling feelings can overcome you, embrace the truth of Psalm 91:2: *"The LORD is* [your] *refuge and fortress."* As you believe and declare this, you will find yourself abiding safely under the shadow of God's presence.

King David often found himself in a place where he could trust nothing and no one except God. He often wrote about this in the psalms. Psalm 20:7 is one of those revealing passages of Scripture that David wrote from his life's experiences. The International Children's Bible translates it (and Psalm 91:2) with childlike faith:

Psalms 20:7 (ICB)

"Some trust in chariots, others in horses. But we trust the Lord our God."

Psalm 91:2b (ICB)

"...You are my place of safety and protection. You are my God, and I trust you."

Before the inevitable storms of life arrive (and they most assuredly will), access the only completely trustworthy, dependable and safe place to be when they do come. When life takes you into places that are beyond tough and they become impossible, only God will make the difference.

With Him, nothing is impossible and all things are possible. Nothing is too difficult for Him. He will see you through to your destiny. Wouldn't it make good sense to occupy such a place on a consistent basis?

Isaiah 26:3-4

"You will keep him in perfect peace, Whose mind is stayed on You, Because he trusts in You. {4} Trust in the LORD forever, For in YAH, the LORD, is everlasting strength."

Things to Think About

1. How would you explain what it means to *"abide"* in a particular place?

2. God graciously gives His people access to His *"secret place."* Have you given Him access to all the places within your heart (especially your secret places)?

3. What or who might you tend to trust, instead of God?

THREE

The Assurance of Deliverance

Psalms 91:3 (NKJV)

"Surely He shall deliver you from the snare of the fowler And from the perilous pestilence."

Psalm 91:3 (GWD)

"He is the one who will rescue you from hunters' traps and from deadly plagues."

This verse promises the sons and daughters of God deliverance from two specific dangers. First, it assures us that the devil and those who devise evil plans towards us will fail. It does this through the imagery of the *"snare"* or net of a *"fowler."*[10] This was a commonly employed method in biblical times to catch or trap birds. Having been trapped, the birds were either killed by the snare or subsequently dispatched when taken from it. Second, Verse 2 inoculates the believer against what the psalmist called *"the perilous"* or *"noisome pestilence."*[11] This refers to a wicked attack of some deadly, life-threatening disease or plague. It also

---

[10] Strong's Numbers H3353 for *"snare"* - from H3369 *"to ensnare"*; H6341 for *"fowler"*.
[11] Strong's Numbers H1942 for *"noisome"* and *"perverse"* or *"very wicked,* - and H1698 for *"pestilence"* or *"plague."*

means some unusual and perverse calamity. The psalmist declared, in full confidence, that these dangers would be walled off from the person who *"abides under the shadow of the Almighty."*

The psalmist intended to assure his readers that a life dedicated to abiding in God is a safe, secure existence. This does not mean that we are completely immune from attack. It does mean that we can stand securely, confident of the deliverance for which we hope. As we are reminded in Hebrews, faith does not ask God how He will do it. It simply declares that He surely will do so. The God's Word Translation of Psalm 91:3 is a great expression of this faith. It simply says, *"He is the one who will rescue you from hunters' traps and from deadly plagues."*

Our Fully Capable Deliverer

There are so many ways to describe the Lord's capabilities to deliver us. He is *"the Most High."* He is omnipotent, omniscient and omnipresent. Let us look at how God described Himself as He was preparing His great deliverance of the children of Israel from their captivity in Egypt.

Exodus 3:7-8, 10, 13-14

> *"And the LORD said: "I have surely seen the oppression of My people who are in Egypt, and have heard their cry because of their taskmasters, for I know their sorrows. {8} So I have come down to deliver them out of the hand of the Egyptians, and to bring them up from that land to a good and*

large land, to a land flowing with milk and honey... {10} Come now, therefore, and I will send you to Pharaoh that you may bring My people, the children of Israel, out of Egypt... {13} Then Moses said to God, "Indeed, when I come to the children of Israel and say to them, 'The God of your fathers has sent me to you,' and they say to me, 'What is His name?' what shall I say to them?" {14} And God said to Moses, "I AM WHO I AM." And He said, "Thus you shall say to the children of Israel, 'I AM has sent me to you.'""

Consider the fundamental difference between *"the fowler,"* who is our adversary the devil, and the great *"I AM."* One is a created, fallen, powerless being, who is a deceiver, liar and thief. The other is God the Creator, who is absolute in faithfulness, infinite in power, and rules over everything. In addition, He loves you with a divine, perfect and unlimited love. *"Surely He shall deliver you from the snare of the fowler."* Nothing can successfully oppose Him or stop Him.

"I AM" was also the supreme statement of Christ's divinity. Jesus used these powerful words to identify Himself in the New Testament.

John 8:58

"Jesus said to them, "Most assuredly, I say to you, before Abraham was, I AM.""

Jesus declared His many attributes as the *"I AM,"* the One who delivers us in every area of life. We will use Jesus' own words from the Book of John to describe Himself. Each of these aspects of His divinity assure of His power to deliver us from the things of this world and into an eternal relationship with Him.

1. *"I am the bread of life."*

   Jesus delivers you from spiritual death.

   John 6:35b

   "...I am the bread of life. He who comes to Me shall never hunger, and he who believes in Me shall never thirst."

   Prior to this first I AM statement, in John, Chapter 6, Jesus had fed five thousand people with five loaves and two small fish. The next day, the people who witnessed this miracle were full of questions. Even thought they had experienced this miracle of divine provision, they did not understand fully who Jesus was. Their thinking about the feeding the five thousand was limited to the actual act of the Lord miraculously providing the bread and fishes. Jesus, knowing what was in their hearts, said the following:

   John 6:26b-27

   "...Most assuredly, I say to you, you seek Me, not because you saw the signs, but because you ate of the loaves and were filled. {27} Do not labor for the food which perishes, but for the food which endures to everlasting life, which the Son of Man will give you, because God the Father has set His seal on Him."

The questions continued. As they asked Jesus for another sign, they were thinking of when God provided *"manna"* in the desert. They were looking for Jesus to fill their bellies with food. The Lord had something far more significant in mind. He turned their reference to *"manna"* into a discussion of His power to deliver His people from hungering for things of this world, into hungering for the everlasting life He was offering them.

John 6:32b-39

"...Most assuredly, I say to you, Moses did not give you the bread from heaven, but My Father gives you the true bread from heaven. {33} For the bread of God is He who comes down from heaven and gives life to the world. {34} Then they said to Him, "Lord, give us this bread always." {35} And Jesus said to them, "I am the bread of life. He who comes to Me shall never hunger, and he who believes in Me shall never thirst. {36} But I said to you that you have seen Me and yet do not believe. {37} All that the Father gives Me will come to Me, and the one who comes to Me I will by no means cast out. {38} For I have come down from heaven, not to do My own will, but the will of Him who sent Me. {39} This is the will of the Father who sent Me, that of all He has given Me I should lose nothing, but should raise it up at the last day."

Jesus often began His words with the expression, *"Most assuredly..."*[12] This was a direct reference to the absolute dependability of what He said, as He spoke of His saving power. Within His words, we find His assurance that He *"should lose nothing."* This meant that all who trust in Him would have a journey safely through life, even as far as eternity. He confirmed this with the following words to His disciples:

John 6:40

"And this is the will of Him who sent Me, that everyone who sees the Son and believes in Him may have everlasting life; and I will raise him up at the last day."

2. *"I am the light of the world."*

Jesus delivers you from darkness and brings you into the light of His presence.

John 8:12

"Then Jesus spoke to them again, saying, "I am the light of the world. He who follows Me shall not walk in darkness, but have the light of life."

This verse speaks of the contrast between light and darkness. Jesus is a gift of light to our darkened world. As we follow Him, navigating our way through our sin-darkened world, our paths will be safely illuminated. There will be no stumbling into the damning and

---

[12] For example, see John 6:26 and John 6:32.

dangerous darkness. As we walk this bright path of faithful followership to Jesus, we will have *"the light of life."* We will have Him. He will have us. This was His direct reference to eternal life with Him. John's report of Jesus' words presents us with a revelatory roadmap of the process of followership, to deliver us from this world; and, take us on our eternal journey all the way to the New Jerusalem. I often have wondered if the Lord had the words of Proverbs 4:18-19 in mind, when He referred to this contrast of light and darkness.

Proverbs 4:18-19

"But the path of the just is like the shining sun, That shines ever brighter unto the perfect day. {19} The way of the wicked is like darkness; They do not know what makes them stumble."

We have all experienced walking in darkness. It may have been physical darkness or perhaps the darkness of fear or uncertainty. Walking in the light of Christ positions us to overcome any kind of darkness; and, have the peace of God as our walking companion. Thank God for Your light, Lord Jesus! We never need to suffer being alone in any form of darkness. You are always there with us.

3. *"I am the door of the sheep."*

Jesus delivers you from *"the thief",* who is Satan.

John 10:7-10

"Then Jesus said to them again, "Most assuredly, I say to you, I am the door of the sheep. {8} All

> *who ever came before Me are thieves and robbers, but the sheep did not hear them. {9} I am the door. If anyone enters by Me, he will be saved, and will go in and out and find pasture. {10} The thief does not come except to steal, and to kill, and to destroy. I have come that they may have life, and that they may have it more abundantly."*"

The *"door of the sheep"* was an easily understood cultural reference. It was a metaphor, a word picture, that those who lived in the agrarian culture of First Century Palestine would have had no trouble understanding. Its meaning would have been clear to everyone. *"I am the door to the sheep"* served as an invitation to those whose hearts would soften. It was an affront to those with hardened hearts, who would ultimately murder Jesus. As He so often did, Jesus followed the declaration of His divine identity with an explanation of the difference between Himself and those who opposed Him.

The choice for those listening was obvious. Follow Jesus and enter into salvation and the blessings of all its provisions; or, reject Him and suffer what that thief, Satan, offered. This choice remains for people today - deliverance or destruction.

4. *"I am the good shepherd."*

Jesus delivers you from vulnerability and destruction.

John 10:11

"I am the good shepherd. The good shepherd gives His life for the sheep."

These words immediately followed Jesus' claim to be *"the door of the sheep."* It was a continuation of the theme recorded in the verses immediately preceding these. It again included a contrast, which reinforced the difference between the destiny He offered and what the devil intended. This was a choice between a *"good shepherd"* and an evil shepherd. The choice seems obvious, but because it involved the free will of those who listened to Jesus, they could choose either.

As it was with *"the door to the sheep,"* Jesus' use of the term, *"good shepherd"* fit in the cultural context of the agrarian times in which He lived. Calling Himself *"the good shepherd"* would have been an obvious reference to the Hebrew Scriptures. It may be reasonable to assume that those who heard His claim to be *"the good shepherd"* were familiar with Psalm 23. This was another challenge to everyone listening. Those who heard Him could accept Him as God... or reject Him as a liar. They could enter into *"the secret place"* or stay exposed to the perils of the world.

Let's look into the contrast that followed the Lord's statement of His deity. John's next verses included a restatement of Jesus' claims. They provided another illustration of the difference between what He offered and what the sinful world offered. From what Jesus said, we can see that He was comparing *"a good shepherd"* with an evil shepherd or *"hireling"* - someone whose motivations had nothing to do with his master's concerns for the sheep.

John 10:12-14

"But a hireling, he who is not the shepherd, one who does not own the sheep, sees the wolf coming and leaves the sheep and flees; and the wolf catches the sheep and scatters them. {13} The hireling flees because he is a hireling and does not care about the sheep. {14} I am the good shepherd; and I know My sheep, and am known by My own."

Psalm 23:1 makes an obvious connection, clearly linking Jesus' claim to be the one about whom David wrote. It was among the most revered of Hebrew Scriptures. I have used the New International Version, because it so clearly illustrates David's personal testimony of his need for Jesus. David declared that, with the *"LORD,"* deliverance was sure.

Psalms 23:1 (NIV)

"A psalm of David. The LORD is my shepherd, I shall not be in want."

5. *"I am the resurrection and the life."*

Jesus delivers you from the fear of death and an eternity without Him.

John 11:25b

"Jesus said to her, "I am the resurrection and the life. He who believes in Me, though he may die, he shall live. {26} And whoever lives and believes in Me shall never die. Do you believe this?""

The historical context of this verse covered the events preceding and including the resurrection of Lazarus. Jesus' question to Martha transcended the natural circumstances in which she found herself. (Natural circumstances have no authority to make demands, when confronted with the person of Jesus Christ.) Jesus proclaimed to Martha that He was bigger than her problem, even if it was the death of her brother, Lazarus. The Lord asked Martha, *"Do you believe this?"* The question became a pivotal point of her life. Even though she had no understanding of the dynamics of what Jesus was about to demonstrate, she loved and believed in Jesus and offered her best. It should be the same in everyone's life. Here is what she said:

John 11:27

"She said to Him, "Yes, Lord, I believe that You are the Christ, the Son of God, who is to come into the world."

"Yes Lord" is an acknowledgement that, even though you have no idea how it will come, deliverance is sure. Cling to your faith in Christ. Then, when your circumstances confront you with the question, *"Do you believe,"* your faith-filled answer of *"Yes Lord"* will secure you through even the most trying circumstances. Your faith-filled response, *"Yes Lord"* illuminates the glory of God. The glory of God manifests His presence and brings His power. With Him, all things are possible and nothing is impossible. What an exciting prospect this is! All it requires is that you believe. *"Surely He will deliver you*

from the snare of the fowler," and bring you into an eternity spent with Him.

John 11:40

"Jesus said to her, "Did I not say to you that if you would believe you would see the glory of God?""

6. *"I am the way, the truth and the life."*

Jesus delivers you from doubt and brings life-giving hope.

John 14:6b

"I am the way, the truth, and the life. No one comes to the Father except through Me."

In response to Thomas's question about how the disciples could know the way to where Jesus was going, the Lord identified Himself as, *"the way the truth, and the life,"* He turned the question into a discourse about the faithfulness of the Father. The Lord knew this knowledge would be vital to His disciples' missions and destiny. They would face persecution, and for most, even death for the cause of Christ. Their hardships would require them to believe God was their source of deliverance and hope.

7. *"I am the true vine."*

Jesus delivers you from a life without fruitfulness or eternal value.

John 15:5

"I am the vine, you are the branches. He who

abides in Me, and I in him, bears much fruit; for without Me you can do nothing."

Jesus used this locally understood imagery of a vine and its branches to illustrate the eternal connection between Him and His followers. This connection was, is and always will be a believer's assurance of his or her eternal position in Christ. The confession that *"surely He will deliver you..."* has substance behind it. It is the Lord's guarantee that God is always there for you, and nothing can disconnect you from Him (except when you choose to do so). Trust that your connection to His abiding presence will deliver you from every snare you may face. A powerful confession in the face of tribulation is simply to say, *"I am connected to the One who is my sure deliverance!"*

John 8:58

"Jesus said to them, "Most assuredly, I say to you, before Abraham was, I AM.""

When Jesus identified Himself as *"I AM,"* He was declaring His eternal divinity.
- He is the one who spoke light into existence.
- He is the one who parted the Red Sea to deliver the people of Israel from four hundred and thirty years of bondage.
- *"I AM"* is the one who consumed Elijah's sacrifice, by sending fire to consume a water-soaked altar of sacrifice, including the rocks that formed its foundations.
- He is the one who empowered a small stone that brought down a giant, delivering the armies of Israel and securing

David's destiny to rule the kingdom.
- He is the spotless Lamb of God, who, having the power to call a legion of angels to Himself at Calvary, had the unfathomable love to stay the course of the cross. Yet, the grave could not hold Him. He is alive and fully God.
- He is the one who will bring judgment and justice to end the reign of sin and Satan. He is Almighty God.

Revelation 19:15

"Now out of His mouth goes a sharp sword, that with it He should strike the nations. And He Himself will rule them with a rod of iron. He Himself treads the winepress of the fierceness and wrath of Almighty God."

He is the *"KING OF KINGS AND LORD OF LORDS."*[13] There can be no doubt. *"Surely He shall deliver you from the snare of the fowler and the perilous pestilence."*

Because of who Jesus is, deliverance is sure!

Things to Think About

1. Why do you suppose there is so much comfort and assurance available from understanding the complete message of the seven *"I AM's"*?
2. Pick your choice of the seven *"I AM's"* and explain why it brings assurance that the believer's deliverance is sure.

---

[13] Revelation 19:16

3. What other sayings of Jesus, when added to the eight times He declared, *"I AM,"* could you use to support the truth that, in Christ, our deliverance is sure?

FOUR
The Wings of Refuge

Psalms 91:4

"He shall cover you with His feathers and under His wings you shall take refuge. His truth shall be your shield and buckler."

In the preceding chapter, you read of the deliverance from the onslaught of the fowler. In Verse 4, the psalmist continued using the poetic imagery of birds. He wrote of the protection that comes from a bird that spreads its wings to cover its vulnerable offspring. As we previously saw, to the people in the agrarian culture of Israel, young birds taking shelter under the wings of a parent was a familiar and easily understood scene.

There were a number of occasions in which God was referred to metaphorically, as having wings. Below, and on the following page are a few of these references.

Psalms 17:8

"Keep me as the apple of Your eye; Hide me under the shadow of Your wings,"

Psalms 36:7

"How precious is Your lovingkindness, O God! Therefore the children of men put their trust under the shadow of Your wings."

Psalms 57:1

"Be merciful to me, O God, be merciful to me! For my soul trusts in You; And in the shadow of Your wings I will make my refuge, Until these calamities have passed by."

Psalms 61:4

"I will abide in Your tabernacle forever; I will trust in the shelter of Your wings. *Selah"*

Psalms 63:7

"Because You have been my help, Therefore in the shadow of Your wings I will rejoice."

The New Testament also contains this imagery of a bird with its young. Jesus applied it to Himself. In Matthew 23:37, Jesus sorrowed over His people, because they had fallen into hardness of heart, and turned their backs on the divine covering they could have enjoyed.

Matthew 23:37

"O Jerusalem, Jerusalem, the one who kills the prophets and stones those who are sent to her! How often I wanted to gather your children

together, as a hen gathers her chicks under her wings, but you were not willing!"

The thematic allusion throughout both testaments was deliberate, consistent and no accident. The Holy Spirit used the preceding Scriptures, and a number of others throughout the Bible, to drive home His point that God keeps us securely *"under His wings."*

"...and under His wings you shall take refuge."

We may amplify the expression *"under His wings"* to become *"under His unfailing wings."* Taking this a step further, we can declare, *"under the unfailing wings of His power and love."* To be covered with God's power and love is to be secure beyond the reach of every evil intention.

The original Hebrew word in Psalm 91:4, which the New King James Version translated, as *"take refuge"* was the word *"chacah"*[14] Strong's Dictionary tells us that in its essence, *"chacah"* means *"to confide in, to make refuge"* or *"to trust."* If we combine this original meaning with what we have just expanded upon, we may paraphrase it this way:

"You can place yourself under God's unfailing covering of protection and refuge. When you do, you can trust Him to keep you safe and secure, as He guards you with His power and love."

---

[14] Strong's Number H2620.

This leads us to two questions.

1. Who initiates the protection described in Verse 4?

2. Who responds to the protection that has been offered; and, what is the response?

The answers to these two questions ought not to be separated. They function as a cooperative effort. The answers overflow with the faithfulness of God, which helps to strengthen our sense of security in Him. Again, Verse 4 says, *"He shall cover you with His feathers and under His wings you shall take refuge."* This tells us that God initiates the protection. He is always watching because He is our Good Shepherd. The verse goes on to say we are to move ourselves from a place of vulnerability to safety under the covering of His wings. This is something we must do in response to God's offer of His divine covering and protection.

His Truth: Spiritual Battle Gear

Psalms 91:4b

"His truth shall be your shield and buckler."

The Bible describes *"truth"* as spiritual battle gear. The Apostle Paul included it in the full armor of God in Ephesians 6. Let's look at the spiritual application of truth as a *"shield;"* and then, as a *"buckler"* or belt.

In biblical Israel, when going into battle, the importance of a warrior's shield could not be overestimated. The Bible provides us with references (Old and New Testament), describing the spiritual value of the *"shield."* In Psalm 91, *"truth"* is described as a *"shield."* In Ephesians 6:16, Paul refers to the *"shield of faith."* Paul placed the shield's importance above all else in the full armor of God. He said this:

Ephesians 6:16

"above all, taking the shield of faith with which you will be able to quench all the fiery darts of the wicked one."

Putting these two descriptions together, we can see the connection between *"truth"* and *"faith"* and the shield they provide us. Let's paraphrase this combination:

"Secure your faith by embracing what God's Word promises, concerning the "truths" you read in it. Allow these "truths" to "shield" or stand between you and the spiritual forces that are arrayed against you. As you do, you will find yourself able to keep standing until you gain your victory."

Now, let's look at what the psalmist called the *"buckler."*

Psalms 91:4b

"His truth shall be your shield and buckler."

Ephesians 6:14a (GWT)

"So then, take your stand! Fasten truth around your waist like a belt."

The God's Word Translation of this verse is, *"Fasten truth around your waist like a belt."* This particular piece of spiritual battle gear has the distinguishing characteristic that it is like a completely dependable *"belt,"* firmly fastened around a person's waist. It provides a sense of security and wholeness. A *"belt of truth"* keeps things in perspective and carries tools of victory, found in the Bible. There is no more powerful weapon than *"truth,"* because it is the revealed Word of God, and is a name for Jesus, Himself.

You can position yourself under *"His wings,"* knowing you have found a secure place from which you can apply those wonderful weapons that He provides for you to be victorious in every battle.

Things to Think About

1. How does positioning yourself under Go's wings impact your relationship with Him?
2. What would stop you from *"embracing what God's Word promises, concerning the "truths" you read in it."* What would help you to embrace His promises?

FIVE

No Fear - Not By Night, Nor By Day

Psalms 91:5-6

"You shall not be afraid of the terror by night, Nor of the arrow that flies by day, {6} Nor of the pestilence that walks in darkness, Nor of the destruction that lays waste at noonday."

Psalms 91:5-6 (NLT)

"Do not be afraid of the terrors of the night, nor fear the dangers of the day, {6} nor dread the plague that stalks in darkness, nor the disaster that strikes at midday."

The psalmist continued to paint an assuring poetic picture of the breadth of covering and safety the Lord provides us. His protection extends to all twenty-four hours of each day. These two verses speak to unknown terrors, unwelcome disease and even catastrophic events. Bad things do happen to God's people. So, why should you fully trust in these verses? To answer this question requires a close look at each of the following four ways to describe threats we might face. We will take them one at a time and unpack their expanded meanings.

1. *"...the terror by night"*

The Hebrew word translated *"terror"* is *"pachad."*[15] Within Israel's historical context, this word would have recalled a sudden, overwhelming feeling of dread or horror, in which the person felt extreme alarm and uncontrollable fear. It speaks of the terror those who might have lived in a simple Israelite village experienced when an enemy came suddenly upon them with violent, evil intent. The psalmist's description of this terror *"by night"* multiplied its impact. It arrived out of the darkness and uncertainties of a night without any light to see it coming. Psalm 91:5 assures us of a secret place that protects us from the unexpected attack of the enemy. We need not live with the emotional dread of these kinds of unknown dangers. Nothing is unknown to God. Always remember that it is His *"secret place."* He is our *"refuge and fortress."* He is our *"very present help in trouble."* He has a wonderfully safe "tree house" just waiting for us, and He will be with us in it.

Psalm 91:2

"I will say of the Lord, He is my refuge and my fortress. My God, in Him I will trust."

Psalms 46:1-3

"God is our refuge and strength, A very present help in trouble. {2} Therefore we will not fear, Even though the earth be removed, And though the mountains be carried into the midst of the sea;

---

[15] Strong's Number H6343.

*{3} Though its waters roar and be troubled,
Though the mountains shake with its swelling.
Selah"*

2. *"Nor of the arrow that flies by day,"*

Imagine a sharply pointed, flying projectile that pierces and fatally wounds its target. The fear of this particular, sudden danger goes beyond our fears of the normal physical weapons of war. It again takes us into the unseen realm of spiritual warfare. Therefore, *"the arrow that flies by day"* may speak of violent, demonic spiritual attacks on God's people. Its meaning is consistent with what the Apostle Paul referred to in Ephesians 6:16 as, *"all the fiery darts of the wicked one."* As we have seen in the previous chapter, faith in the One who provides you a secret place of safety is the key to quenching or neutralizing *"all"* these *"fiery darts."*

Ephesians 6:16

"above all, taking the shield of faith with which you will be able to quench all the fiery darts of the wicked one."

3. *"Nor of the pestilence that walks in darkness,"*

The simplest way to express the meaning of *"pestilence,"* is in terms of an unstoppable plague that destroys the lives it infects. The New Living Translation describes it as the *"the plague that stalks in darkness."* This gives us the idea that it is not a random contagion, but is a deadly disease that picks its victims and stalks them with deliberate malice and intent. The psalmist wrote not to be afraid of it. God is bigger than any disease. His protection can both keep us from it and if necessary, provide the miracle that destroys the stalker and heals us.

4. *"Nor of the destruction that lays waste at noonday."*

This statement presents a picture that implies devastation, complete ruin and the collapse of peaceful order into chaos. This is not a hidden attack, springing from the darkness, but one that arrogantly offers its evil in the light of the midday sun. It does its damage in the height of brightness, for all to see. It does not try to hide its misery-producing work. It leaves a complete wasteland in its wake. Nothing of value remains to salvage. This is an accurate picture of the end game or goal of the devil. It is an "in your face" assault on our faith and the belief that God is able to keep us from it. However, the psalmist has declared that we shall not be afraid of it.

I have learned to keep Psalm 91 so close to my heart that when bad things happen (and they will), I try to turn immediately to Psalm 91's reassuring words. With authority, they demand that my fears submit to my trust in the Lord. It may take some effort and work to gain agreement with this demand; but knowing that every word of Scripture is true ultimately gets me through the problem and into my victory.

God Will Prevail.

Romans 8:31

"What then shall we say to these things? If God is for us, who can be against us?"

What are we to take away from Romans 8:31? God is with us and regardless of what is against us, He will prevail. *"What shall we say"*? I suggest we say loudly and repeatedly, *"Our test will become our testimony, in Jesus mighty name;"* ...and, we say this while still in the midst of the test. I have found that a word of faith will not only speak to my problem, but perhaps more importantly, to my ability to cling to God, and get beyond my fear and move into action.

Your Response: A Question of Faith

What was the Lord's response when His disciples became fearful? We can answer this with a number of examples in the Gospels. However, we have one narrative that helps greatly in understanding His grace-filled care for us. In the Scriptures that follow, you will see that Jesus stepped in the way of the threat and stripped it of its power. Then, He asked His disciples why they were so fearful. Why didn't they handle the threat themselves? They could not see that they had God-given authority over their fears. They even had power, through their faith, to calm their own storms. Here is the narrative that holds this lesson:

Mark 4:35-40

"On the same day, when evening had come, He said to them, "Let us cross over to the other side." {36} Now when they had left the multitude, they took Him along in the boat as He was. And other little boats were also with Him. {37} And a great windstorm arose, and the waves beat into the

boat, so that it was already filling. {38} But He was in the stern, asleep on a pillow. And they awoke Him and said to Him, "Teacher, do You not care that we are perishing?" {39} Then He arose and rebuked the wind, and said to the sea, "Peace, be still!" And the wind ceased and there was a great calm. {40} But He said to them, "Why are you so fearful? How is it that you have no faith?""

Some of Jesus' disciples were seasoned fishermen. They had probably ridden out many such windstorms on the Sea of Galilee. Nevertheless, fear gripped all of them. They did not understand the power they had been given to overcome such circumstances. They did not exercise their own faith; otherwise, they would not have had to awaken the Master. When they did wake Him, He simply commanded the storm raging around them to be still. Then Jesus said to His disciples, *"Why are you so fearful?"* What He was saying may be paraphrased as follows:

> *"Do you not know the power I have given you to overcome the fear of your circumstances?"*

Listen to the voice of the Master. He said, *"Peace, be still."* Learn to say it to yourself. Then be sure to say it to your storm. Fear will only work its destruction if you accept it and allow it to have a home in your heart. The way Satan gets you to give fear a home is to convince you that it belongs to you, and you belong to it. The devil wages this battle in the arena of your mind.

2 Corinthians 10:3-5

"For though we walk in the flesh, we do not war according to the flesh. {4} For the weapons of our warfare are not carnal but mighty in God for pulling down strongholds, {5} casting down arguments and every high thing that exalts itself against the knowledge of God, bringing every thought into captivity to the obedience of Christ,"

You increase your faith by meditating on God's Word.

Romans 10:17

"So then faith comes by hearing, and hearing by the word of God."

Similarly, you can increase your fear by meditating on the lies that bring you terror, flaming darts, sickness and finally, destruction. We could accurately say this:

"Fear comes by hearing and accepting evil reports, listening to your own thoughts of defeat, or accepting the lies that say you will not overcome. Ultimately, fear comes by not trusting God."

It is your choice. Position yourself right now under His wings; and, think about His goodness.

Psalm 31:19-20a

"Oh, how great is Your goodness, Which You have prepared for those who trust in You in the presence of the sons of men! {20} You shall hide them in the secret place of Your presence..."

Things to Think About

1. Why do you think fear has such power?

2. Why would the thought of darkness so easily bring the emotion of fear? What would be your suggestion for overcoming fear in the night?

3. In this chapter, you read that The New Living Translation described *"pestilence"* as, the *"the plague that stalks in darkness."* This presented the idea that sickness is not a random contagion, but a deliberate, evil targeting of a person. Do you believe that sickness can be a result of a demonic attack? Discuss why this would or would not be reality in the world in which you live?

SIX
Stop Counting. Start Believing.

Psalm 91:7-8

"A thousand may fall at your side, And ten thousand at your right hand; But it shall not come near you. {8} Only with your eyes shall you look, And see the reward of the wicked."

One of the highly effective writing techniques of Hebrew poetry was the use of hyperbole, which is deliberate exaggeration for effect. In Verse 7, the psalmist again used this literary technique to emphasize his point of divine protection even more strongly. This brought strength to what the psalmist said. Below, is my paraphrase of the first part of Verse 7:

"Many may fall (even multitudes), as they become victim to the things they fear. However, in spite of what seems to leave you alone and insignificant among many, God guarantees that if you will position yourself under the shadow of His wings, and place your trust completely in Him, He will keep the trouble from you."

The exaggeration and repetition in Verse 7a was a deliberately focused, powerful insertion. It was written to make a point about trust. There is to be no doubt that trusting in God is a personal choice. It transcends whatever the events around us may try to dictate to us, no matter how desperate or overwhelming they may seem. The idea of trusting God by positioning ourselves under the shadow of His wings is also found in Psalm 36:5-7. Here again, the psalmist emphasized the principle that proximity to God is safety.

Psalm 36:5-7

"Your mercy, O LORD, is in the heavens; Your faithfulness reaches to the clouds. {6} Your righteousness is like the great mountains; Your judgments are a great deep; O LORD, You preserve man and beast. {7} How precious is Your lovingkindness, O God! Therefore the children of men put their trust under the shadow of Your wings."

Beyond the Reach of Circumstances

God is able to suspend or cancel natural circumstances that bring you fear. He does this in many ways, but each will take you beyond the reach of your circumstances. He will walk you successfully through them, or He will shelter you from them. Trusting God is an act of faith, which is a force that should not be underestimated. When faith is at work in you, it will become a power at work around you. This happens because God responds to your faith, and will shower you with His favor, protection, blessings and love. When you accepted Christ as Lord and Savior, He came to live in you and provide you with the faith you need, when you need it. You simply need to believe and then use what He has provided.

> *Ephesians 3:20-21*
>
> *"Now to Him who is able to do exceedingly abundantly above all that we ask or think, according to the power that works in us, {21} to Him be glory in the church by Christ Jesus to all generations, forever and ever. Amen."*

Believing is Seeing.

In the previous chapter, I referred to an "in your face" assault on your faith by the evil that invites you to fear it. The psalmist wrote that multitudes may fall and perish, but as you trust God, you will remain secure. Verse 8 says you will be an eyewitness, standing and looking at the wicked, as they fall before the hand of God that moves to protect you.

> *Psalm 91:8*
>
> *"Only with your eyes shall you look, And see the reward of the wicked."*

The Hebrew word translated by the New King James Version as *"reward"* is *"shillumah"*[16] In the context of Psalm 91, it may be translated appropriately as *"retribution."* This term is synonymous with *"reckoning"* or *"justice."* God promised that He will bring His retribution on the wicked who rise against you. Be sure to

---

[16] Strong's Number H8011.

understand that these verses are conditional. For them to be effective, they require you to exercise trust.

Psalm 91:7-8 has historical roots in the way warfare was conducted in biblical Palestine. Old Testament narratives told of the practice of kings going into battle with their armies. An example of this is found in 2 Kings 3. It recorded the kings of Israel, Judah and Edom going with their armies into the desert to fight against the rebellious Moabites. The kings and their armies experienced a miracle, in which God filled desert ditches with water to save them from dying of thirst. In addition, the Moabites, because of the shining of the sun, mistook the water for blood. Losing heart, the Moabites fled the battlefield.

Perhaps the best-known example of kings going into battle is found in 1 Samuel 17. It recorded King Saul and his army facing the Philistines and their champion, Goliath of Gath. The Israelites were paralyzed with fear of *"the destruction that lays waste at noonday."* When David came upon the battle, he saw Goliath and heard the giant's blasphemous boasts. David boldly went into the valley to face him. David had total disregard for the words or the weapons of the giant. David confronted Goliath, saying he (David) came in the name of the Lord. Then, David prophesied to Goliath that he would take the giant's head off. David valiantly embraced his faith and refused to fear. God packaged the power of David's faith into a small, ordinary stone. Then, God anointed the stone. With it, David killed the giant.

A third example of kings going into battle is found in 2 Samuel 21:15-17. It recorded King David's final time leading his army in battle against the Philistines. David's advanced age had caught up with him. Goliath's son, Ishbi-Benob, who was also a giant, stood over David and was about to slay him. In that moment, God provided Abishai, David's faithful warrior chieftain, to meet David's need. Abishai stepped in and killed the giant.

All three narratives verified the principles that the child of God can *"Trust in the LORD with all your heart,"* (Proverbs 3:5a) and then, expect that, *"No weapon formed against you shall prosper,"* (Isaiah 54:17a). These principles remain true today. They continue to give evidence that *"A thousand may fall at your side, And ten thousand at your right hand; But it shall not come near you..."*

It would be important at this point to remind you that Verses 7-8 of Psalm 91 are conditional. Regardless of what you may face, the singularly important condition is that you have committed your ways to trusting God. Then, you can expect to enjoy His promise of deliverance when trouble arrives. Another place in the Bible where we may find verification of this principle is in Psalm 37:5-6.

Psalm 37:5-6

"Commit your way to the LORD, Trust also in Him, And He shall bring it to pass. {6} He shall bring forth your righteousness as the light, And your justice as the noonday."

We are assured that we will be eyewitnesses to God's response to our commitment and trust, as He steps between the threats and us. This was the psalmist's inspired pledge to his readers, and to us.

Eyes of Faith

It has been said that, *"Seeing is believing."* This may be true in a natural sense. However, those of us who set our minds on *"things of the Spirit"* (Romans 8:5) commit to and trust in the Holy Spirit for guidance and understanding. We are standing on the principle we are seeing in this chapter that *"Believing is seeing."*

Perhaps, as I did over thirteen years ago, you have experienced a life-condemning doctor's report. You might have seen the x-rays or scans and listened to a negative prognosis. There it may have been a condemning image in black and white, accompanied by the doctor's educated, expert opinion. This would have left you with two choices. The first was to believe the apparent inevitability of what you saw and heard. The second, however, was to see what you believed through the eyes of faith; and, reject anything that disagreed with the promises of God. Even if you had seen countless others submit to the apparent inevitability of their doctors' reports you chose to believe God. Experience has taught me (and perhaps you too) simply to believe, and then receive and submit to God's report.

In 2 Chronicles 20, Jehoshaphat, the King of Judah, received a threatening, discouraging report that the people of Ammon, along with others who joined them, were coming to do battle against him and his people. Jehoshapat was facing great odds. It looked grim. However, in the midst of his fear, Jehoshaphat's immediate reaction upon hearing this bad report was to *"set himself to seek the LORD."* It is a model for us to emulate.

> *2 Chronicles 20:3*
>
> *"And Jehoshaphat feared, and set himself to seek the LORD, and proclaimed a fast throughout all Judah."*

As Jehoshaphat and the congregation stood in the house of the Lord, the Spirit of God came upon a man named Jahaziel. He prophesied the following:

> *2 Chronicles 20:15*
>
> *"...Listen, all you of Judah and you inhabitants of Jerusalem, and you, King Jehoshaphat! Thus says the LORD to you: 'Do not be afraid nor dismayed because of this great multitude, for the battle is not yours, but God's.'"*

When you have faith to believe what you may not yet see, God will confirm that your battle has become His. Then, you can *"stand still and see the salvation of the Lord."* This was a sure word to King Jehoshaphat, and it is the same for you. Jahaziel continued his prophetic word in this manner:

> *2 Chronicles 20:17*
>
> *"'You will not need to fight in this battle. Position yourselves, stand still and see the salvation of the LORD, who is with you, O Judah and Jerusalem!' Do not fear or be dismayed; tomorrow go out against them, for the LORD is with you."*

It is all a matter of positioning. Put yourself in that *"secret place of the Most High."* Stand still and allow your heart to draw closer to God. Wait for a word from Him. Then believe, get moving, go out, and see His word become reality. The Bible says that, in the morning, Jehoshaphat and his people went out and began to sing and praise. The LORD set ambushes against their enemies, who became so confused that they fought and destroyed each other (2 Chronicles 20:22-23). This was another biblical example that, though *"A thousand may fall at your side,"* the question will always be, whose report will you believe? Jehoshaphat and his people believed God and subsequently rejoiced over the outcomes of the battle. The last report was God's report.

2 Chronicles 20:30

"Then the realm of Jehoshaphat was quiet, for his God gave him rest all around."

Below, I have illustrated four steps in the process in which the principle of *"Believing is seeing"* works.

1. Position yourself in *"the secret place of the Most High."*
2. Believe what God has said. Stand still and watch for Him to move.
3. Before, during and after the crisis, continue to behave in obedience to His Word. At the appropriate time, go out and do what you must do. Do it with praise on your lips and thanksgiving in your heart.
4. Rejoice over the results. Enjoy your victory in the LORD. (You may want to do so at the start of the battle, as your

personal declaration that *"Believing is seeing."*)

Things to Think About

1. Consider what it means to position yourself under God's wing. How would you explain this to someone?
2. In this chapter, you read the following: "When faith is at work in you, it will become a power at work around you." How would you explain this to a person who has little or no experience with God?
3. Convert *"No weapon formed against you will prosper"* (Isaiah 54:17) into language you would use to explain it to an unbeliever.
4. How would you explain the advantages of faithfully serving God, when bad things happen?

Paraphrase of the First Section of Psalm 91: God is our Refuge.

Verses 1-8

"Whoever quietly and constantly remains at rest in that hidden place in God, will be comfortably at home, secure in his relationship with the One who is above all others, and has the power to guarantee security, safety and peace. {2} I will say of the LORD (I will not keep silent) He is my protection and a wall between me and whatever wants to harm me.

{3} surely, without any doubt or hesitation, the LORD will prevent you from being trapped and destroyed like a bird in the cage of a fowler. He will even stop the perils and wicked attacks of deadly, life-threatening diseases or plagues. This holds true for unusual and perverse calamities.

{4} Caring for you as an eagle cares for its young, God will place you under the unfailing wings of His power and love. You will be secure beyond the reach of any evil intent. This means when you place yourself under the unfailing covering of God's protection and refuge, you can trust Him to keep you safe and secure, as He brings life to your hopes, dreams and visions.

{5} Have no fear of the unknown that may come out of the darkness and uncertainties of a night without any light to see it coming. God will protect you from the sudden, unseen dangers of

demonic spiritual activities. {6} He will also stop both random contagion and disease that pick their victim with deliberate malice and intent. Even when attempts an "in your face" assault on your faith, God will be there to move into the assault on your behalf.

{7} Many may fall (even multitudes), as they become victim to the things they fear. However, in spite of what seems to leave you a lone, insignificant person among many, God guarantees that when you position yourself under the shadow of His wings, and place your trust completely in Him, He will keep the trouble at a distance from you. {8} Believe and trust in the LORD. You will be an eyewitness to the destruction of what has tried to destroy you.

Part Two: He Shall Give His Angels Charge Over You.
Verses 9-13

SEVEN

Possessor of Heaven and Earth

Psalm 91:9-10

"Because you have made the LORD, who is my refuge, Even the Most High, your dwelling place, {10} No evil shall befall you, Nor shall any plague come near your dwelling;"

As he did in Verse 1, the psalmist identified *"the LORD"* as *"the Most High,"* the person in the supreme or highest position. Nobody had more power and authority. Nobody was His equal. This will never change. The psalmist then called *"the LORD"* *"your dwelling place."* This is the Hebrew word, *"ohel"*[17] which means, *"an abode, of God; a retreat"* or *"habitation."* This carried forward the theme that God was both the protector and the place of protection. From this, we understand that He is all we need to keep us safe. From the context of the psalm, it is clear that this *"dwelling place"* not only referred to a place in which to be secured and protected, but also designated a home in which one could dwell with the LORD.

In Verses 9-10, the psalmist displayed the technique of cause and effect.[18] This is clearly illustrated in the New

---

[17] Strong's Number H4168.
[18] As in so many of the verses in Psalm 91, this is synthetic parallelism.

International Version, in which an *"IF - THEN"* relationship is used.

> Cause - Verse 9:
>
> *"IF you make the lord your dwelling..."*
>
> Effect - Verse 10:
>
> *"THEN no harm will befall you, no disaster will come near your tent."*

The word *"befall,"* should not be understood to have indicated an accidental or unintentional misfortune. The original Hebrew word translated as *"befall"* was *"anah."*[19] Its original meaning was, *"to meet someone or approach them for the purpose of seeking a quarrel."*

I have paraphrased Verses 9-10 in the following way:

> *"The LORD, who is above all, reigns in sovereign majesty. Because you have chosen to make Him your abiding place (as I have), no intent to harm you shall be allowed to approach the place in which you dwell. {10} No evil that intentionally seeks a quarrel with you, in order to hurt you, will have the freedom to do so. God will protect you."*

The assurances Verses 9-10 gave ought to be enough for people of faith. Too often, however, they are not. Doubt and unbelief do not readily accept God's promise that He will do what He said He would do. Doubt and unbelief demand to

---

[19] Strong's Number H579.

be provided with an explanation of how God will work His grace and mercy. This demand is a classic example of our human nature trying to insist on a natural explanation that will justify a spiritually-initiated move of God. This is an unreasonable, unacceptable challenge to God. We cannot demand that He explain Himself. It is a test that God does not allow. He will not answer the demand. God will reverse the test and ask us to challenge our own faith. Faith is always the foundation of the test.

The writer could have ended Psalm 91 with these two verses. They say enough to fill a library of faith. They provided us with all the assurances we need, without having to justify the truth they deliver.

"Even the Most High"
(Verse 9)

Depending on which English translation we access, the expression *"Most High"* (*"elyown elyown"*) appears about fifty times in the Bible. Its first three occurrences came in Genesis 14:18-20, which provided the narrative of Abram's tithe to Melchizedek.[20] In these verses, Melchizedek was called *"the priest of God Most High."*

In Genesis 14:19, God's name was expressed as *"God Most High, Possessor of heaven and earth."* This tells us that heaven and earth belong to the *"Most High."* God is

---

[20] The Hebrew name Melchizedek means King of Righteousness. The author accepts that, from the whole counsel of the Bible, this described Jesus. Further confirmation of Melchizedek's identity as Jesus comes from Hebrews 5:5-10. It described Him *"as High Priest according to the order of Melchizedek."*

supreme. All His creation belongs to Him. When we go to that *"secret place"* for refuge, we go to *"the Most High,"* who possesses all of His creation. Nothing could be more assuring and comforting. Our love has possessed God and in turn, His love has possessed us. What a combination!

Below, I have provided you with a sampling of Scriptures. Each of these confirms the power and authority of the *"Most High,"* who is the *"Possessor of heaven and earth."*

Genesis 14:18-20

"Then Melchizedek king of Salem brought out bread and wine; he was the priest of God Most High. {19} And he blessed him and said: "Blessed be Abram of God Most High, Possessor of heaven and earth; {20} And blessed be God Most High, Who has delivered your enemies into your hand." And he gave him a tithe of all. {21} Now the king of Sodom said to Abram, "Give me the persons, and take the goods for yourself." {22} But Abram said to the king of Sodom, "I have raised my hand to the LORD, God Most High, the Possessor of heaven and earth,"

Psalms 18:13

"The LORD also thundered in the heaven, And the Most High uttered His voice, Hailstones and coals of fire."

Psalms 21:7

"For the king trusts in the LORD, And through the mercy of the Most High he shall not be moved."

Daniel 3:26

"Then Nebuchadnezzar went near the mouth of the burning fiery furnace and spoke, saying, "Shadrach, Meshach, and Abed-Nego, servants of the Most High God, come out, and come here." Then Shadrach, Meshach, and Abed-Nego came from the midst of the fire."

The experience of Daniel's three friends in the fiery furnace illustrated that faithfulness to God always takes priority. God will respond to interrupt the circumstances; but, even when it seems He has not done so, do not waver in your faith. Your faithfulness to God will always take you beyond your circumstances. There is a hope and a future with which to keep your heart filled with faith.

The Issue of Power and Authority

Isaiah 14:12-15

"How you are fallen from heaven, O Lucifer, son of the morning! How you are cut down to the ground, You who weakened the nations! {13} For you have said in your heart: 'I will ascend into heaven, I will exalt my throne above the stars of God; I will also sit on the mount of the congregation On the farthest sides of the north; {14} I will ascend above the heights of the clouds,

> *I will be like the Most High.' {15} Yet you shall be brought down to Sheol, To the lowest depths of the Pit."*

A self-serving desire for power and authority has been the cause of evil from the very beginning. There have been no exceptions. It caused *"the Most High"* to throw Satan down from heaven for coveting what belonged exclusively to the Lord. He did so because Satan presumed to be just like Him, equal in power and authority. It was pure rebellion. In the Garden of Eden, Eve was tempted by the serpent to disregard God's authority, by eating from the tree of the knowledge of good and evil. Adam then abandoned his responsibility to exercise his delegated authority. He submitted to the lies of the serpent, that devil Satan, and rebelled. From that point until today, refusal to submit to legitimate power and authority (or the misuse of it) has continued to reflect humanity's fallen state of rebellion. It is the exercise and evidence of sin. One day, there will be thrones of judgment; and, Satan will be cast into eternal torment as judgment for his rebellion against *"the Most High."*

Revelation 20:7-10

> *"Now when the thousand years have expired, Satan will be released from his prison {8} and will go out to deceive the nations which are in the four corners of the earth, Gog and Magog, to gather them together to battle, whose number is as the sand of the sea. {9} They went up on the breadth of the earth and surrounded the camp of the saints and the beloved city. And fire came down from*

God out of heaven and devoured them. {10} The devil, who deceived them, was cast into the lake of fire and brimstone where the beast and the false prophet are. And they will be tormented day and night forever and ever."

Those who have faithfully refused to bend to Satan's temptation to rebel against God will have eternal joy in the presence of *"God Most High."* Then, *"the secret place"* will no longer be necessary. Everything will be open and in the light. There will be no more darkness or evil. It will have gone to its place as part of the second death, in the lake of fire. All those who clung to a sinful, self-serving desire for power and authority will also burn in the lake of fire. Those who have lived faithfully for Christ will continue in His presence for eternity, without end.

Revelation 22:1-5

"And he showed me a pure river of water of life, clear as crystal, proceeding from the throne of God and of the Lamb. {2} In the middle of its street, and on either side of the river, was the tree of life, which bore twelve fruits, each tree yielding its fruit every month. The leaves of the tree were for the healing of the nations. {3} And there shall be no more curse, but the throne of God and of the Lamb shall be in it, and His servants shall serve Him. {4} They shall see His face, and His name shall be on their foreheads. {5} There shall be no night there: They need no lamp nor light of the

sun, for the Lord God gives them light. And they shall reign forever and ever."

Things to Think About

1. Verses 9-10 could fill a library of faith. What New Testament Scriptures would you select to expand this library? (Select at least four.)

2. How can you guard yourself from rebelling against God, even in the smallest way?

EIGHT

In the Care of Angels

Psalm 91:11-12 (NKJV)

"For He shall give His angels charge over you, To keep you in all your ways. {12} In their hands they shall bear you up, Lest you dash your foot against a stone."

Psalms 91:11 (NLT)

"For he orders his angels to protect you wherever you go."

Psalms 91:11 (NIV)

"For he will command his angels concerning you to guard you in all your ways;"

A *"charge"* is a command given by a superior authority. For it to be effective, those who are commanded to carry out the charge must act upon it. Verse 11 tells us that the Creator and Sustainer of the universe shall command His angels to provide those *"in the secret place"* with divinely supervised and empowered protection. His angels will be your supernaturally superior guardians. They will faithfully honor and fulfill their *"charge."* They will *"keep you in all of your ways."* Verse 11 is God's assurance that the angels will be able to do so, regardless of circumstances. The next verse metaphorically stated how they would do this.

Psalm 91:12

"In their hands they shall bear you up, Lest you dash your foot against a stone."

I have paraphrased Verses 11-12. It is followed by Jude's doxology, which makes a wonderful devotional ending to the paraphrase.

"These angels, on assignment from "God Most High," will take a "hands-on-approach" to what He has commanded them to do. {12} They will be your angelic defenders, upholding you, as God, Himself would. Their faithful actions will keep you from stumbling into or against whatever is placed before you to harm you. It will be as if the Lord Jesus Christ is stepping between you and your enemies, as He invades your circumstances or trouble."

Jude 24-25

"Now to Him who is able to keep you from stumbling, And to present you faultless Before the presence of His glory with exceeding joy, {25} To God our Savior, Who alone is wise, Be glory and majesty, Dominion and power, Both now and forever. Amen."

The reassurances that Psalm 91 provide make a significant contribution to the issue of having faith in God. In Verse 12 of the psalm, the original Hebrew word for *"bear"* is *"nasa."*[21] Other English language translations of this word are *"carry," "catch," "lift,"* and *"hold."* The symbolism is obvious. The angels' actions will keep you from stumbling and being hurt by what you have stumbled against.

Reflect again on the beginning sentences of my earlier paraphrase of Psalm 91:11-12:

> *"These angels, on assignment from "God Most High," will take a "hands-on-approach" to what He has commanded them to do. They will be your supporting and covering angelic defenders, upholding you, as God, Himself would."*

His angels will support, cover and uphold you. These words denote deliberate, steadfast action by His angels. I encourage you to believe and be in agreement with what these words have said. It is a fully dependable fact.

The "Master's Guests"

As I was recently reading from The Treasury of David, I could not get beyond the words of Charles Spurgeon, concerning Verses 11-12. He wrote of the rich promises in these two verses, as only Spurgeon could. Allow his words to speak to you as powerfully as they spoke to me.

---

[21] Strong's Number H5375.

"*"For he shall give his angels charge over thee."*

Not one guardian angel, as some fondly dream, but all the angels are here alluded to in this verse. They are the bodyguard of the princes of the blood imperial of heaven, and they have received commission from their Lord and ours to watch carefully over all the interests of the faithful… It is down to the marching orders of the hosts of heaven that they take special note of the people who dwell in God. It is not to be wondered at that the servants are bidden to be careful of the comfort of their Master's guests; and we may be quite sure that when they are specially charged by the Lord himself they will carefully discharge the duty imposed upon them…. to be a bodyguard, a garrison to the body, soul, and spirit of the saint… Perhaps we shall one day stand amazed at the multiplied services, which the unseen bands have rendered to us.

"They shall bear thee up in their hands"; as nurses carry little children, with careful love, so shall those glorious spirits upbear each individual believer, desirable that we should not stumble, but as the way is rough, it is most gracious on the Lord's part to send his servants to bear us up above the loose pebbles… it shows the wisdom of the Lord that from the smaller evils we are protected."[22]

---

[22] Spurgeon, Charles H., <u>The Treasury of David, Volume Two</u>, Hendrickson Publishers, Peabody, Mass, P.93.

The "Master's guests" enjoy complete confidence that *"A thousand may fall"* around His dwelling place, but within it, every guest is secure. In addition, the Master extends His hand of companionship and communion. Have you thought about this? Have you considered how incredibly special it is to be the guest of God? As His guest in residence in *"the secret place,"* you can join your brothers and sisters in the Lord to say, "Even from the smaller evils we are protected."[23]

Your perfect Savior is concerned that you, as His guest, will be perfectly cared for in His dwelling place. He makes perfect provision for your comfort. His gift to you upon your entry into His *"secret place"* is that you immediately become welcome to stay as long as you desire, even up to and including eternity!

A Conditional Covenant

The Holy Spirit inspired the writer of Psalm 91 to follow Verses 9-10 with Verses 11-12. This was a strategic choice.

Psalms 91:9-12

"Because you have made the LORD, who is my refuge, Even the Most High, your dwelling place, {10} No evil shall befall you, Nor shall any plague come near your dwelling; {11} For He shall give His angels charge over you, To keep you in all your ways. {12} In their hands they shall bear you up, Lest you dash your foot against a stone."

---

[23] Quoted from Spurgeon, above. See the footnote, bottom of Page 72.

In these verses, the formula for God's faithful care has been presented in a powerfully effective package. It guarantees that, as long as you inhabit God's *"secret place,"* He will put angels on alert to guard your path and take you to your destiny. In return for this promise of angelic care, guidance and protection, God asks you to commit to making *"the secret place"* your dwelling place. There, you can abide peacefully in the midst of any storm, fully trusting Him. This takes us back to the second verse of Psalm 91, in which the psalmist said, *"...in Him will I trust."* This is a major theme of the entire psalm. God is completely trustworthy. There are no exceptions.

God's promise to place you in the hands of His angels, coupled with your corresponding commitment to abide with Him in His *"secret place,"* creates a conditional covenant to insure your safety and security. God will not break His end of the covenant. It is our responsibility to do our part.

Things to Think About

1. Charles Spurgeon wrote, "Perhaps we shall one day stand amazed at the multiplied services which the unseen bands have rendered to us." Is there anything God's angels might have done for you that you considered simply chance happenings? Try to recall one such occasion. How did His unseen band of angels actually change things for you?

2. In this chapter I wrote, "As His guest in residence in *"the secret place,"* you can join your brothers and sisters in the Lord to say, "Even from the smaller evils we are protected."" We do not always recognize "the smaller

evils" for what they are. Can you think of an encounter with these evils that did not seem overly important, but as God stepped in, the situation turned to something unexpectedly good?

NINE

Trampled Underfoot

Psalm 91:13 (NKJV)

"You shall tread upon the lion and the cobra, The young lion and the serpent you shall trample underfoot."

Psalms 91:13 (KJV)

"Thou shalt tread upon the lion and adder: the young lion and the dragon shalt thou trample under feet."

"The young lion and the dragon" represent the fierceness of the dangers we may face. The imagery is repeated and exaggerated, giving it more emphasis and force. The description of treading on lions, snakes and dragons paints a powerfully symbolic picture. However, it ought not to be taken as an invitation to go into the wilderness and test its literal truthfulness. To attempt to do so would be presumption. It most likely would have an unhappy result. As you read earlier, we are not to test God (or His Word). The opposite is true. God tests us to help us see if we will fully trust Him, under the shelter of His divine protection. [24]

---

[24] The only exception to this rule, would be tithes and offerings (Malachi 3:8).

The Hebrew word translated *"serpent"* in the New King James is *"tanniyn."*[25] Its meanings included a marine or land monster, sea serpent, jackal... or, (as in the King James Version) a *"dragon."* This term *"dragon"* opens up some additionally interesting meanings that fit with the nature of the verse. The biblical term *"dragon"* has both natural and theological implications. Without reading a specific intention into what was not literally stated, might we apply this term, as I have paraphrased it, below?

Paraphrase of Psalm 91:13

"You shall stomp and trample underfoot whatever evils endanger you. You shall walk safely beyond the threats of Satan, who is that dragon of old, the devil. You shall see the efforts of whoever or whatever desires to devour you (including all the schemes of the devil) become your stepping stones to victory."

The latter part of the verse, in the New King James Version says, *"...and the serpent you shall trample underfoot."* Among the ways *"trample"* may be defined are, *"to domineer harshly; crush... To put out or extinguish by trampling."*[26] This is much more than simply stepping on your problems. It is inflicting crushing, fatal damage on them. As you trust God, and place yourself in close fellowship with Him, He will empower you to trample or extinguish the threat. You will have the opportunity, by faith, to take personal action in concert with God. He will

---

[25] Strong's Number H8577.
[26] Random House Webster's College Dictionary.

put the devil and his agents under your feet.

Romans 16:20

"And the God of peace will crush Satan under your feet shortly. The grace of our Lord Jesus Christ be with you. Amen."

The Rest of the Story… All the Way to the End

The Book of Revelation has already confirmed the devil's end. It will come at the hand of Almighty God. In the meantime, your battles will not be fought alone. You will have angelic support to gain each victory. Below are examples from the Book of Revelation, assuring you of being on the winning team. You will have your battles, but ultimately, God Himself will finish the enmity that started when He cast Satan from heaven. In the end, God will destroy that evil *"dragon"* and his fallen angels.

Revelation 12:9

"So the great dragon was cast out, that serpent of old, called the Devil and Satan, who deceives the whole world; he was cast to the earth, and his angels were cast out with him."

Revelation 20:1-3, 7-10

"Then I saw an angel coming down from heaven, having the key to the bottomless pit and a great chain in his hand. {2} He laid hold of the dragon, that serpent of old, who is the Devil and Satan, and bound him for a thousand years; {3} and he

cast him into the bottomless pit, and shut him up, and set a seal on him, so that he should deceive the nations no more till the thousand years were finished. But after these things he must be released for a little while... {7} Now when the thousand years have expired, Satan will be released from his prison {8} and will go out to deceive the nations which are in the four corners of the earth, Gog and Magog, to gather them together to battle, whose number is as the sand of the sea. {9} They went up on the breadth of the earth and surrounded the camp of the saints and the beloved city. And fire came down from God out of heaven and devoured them. {10} The devil, who deceived them, was cast into the lake of fire and brimstone where the beast and the false prophet are. And they will be tormented day and night forever and ever."

Have confidence in God and His plan. You are a vital part of it. As a committed believer, you will be with the armies of heaven when Christ returns (Revelation 19:7-8, 19:14). You will witness the end of Satan's attempts to usurp God's authority. You will be there when the final battle is won and judgment is carried out. Satan, his demons and all who chose to serve the creature and not the Creator will be burning in the lake of fire. Then, you will not need the *"secret place"* any more. You will abide for all eternity in the New Jerusalem, where there can be no darkness or evil - only peace, health and light.

Revelation 22:1-5

"And he showed me a pure river of water of life, clear as crystal, proceeding from the throne of God and of the Lamb. {2} In the middle of its street, and on either side of the river, was the tree of life, which bore twelve fruits, each tree yielding its fruit every month. The leaves of the tree were for the healing of the nations. {3} And there shall be no more curse, but the throne of God and of the Lamb shall be in it, and His servants shall serve Him. {4} They shall see His face, and His name shall be on their foreheads. {5} There shall be no night there: They need no lamp nor light of the sun, for the Lord God gives them light. And they shall reign forever and ever."

The confidence we have in Him is that our abiding place for all eternity is secure because of His prophetic promise for our future. He is always ready to perform His Word. He is forever faithful.

Things to Think About

1. You read that, among the ways the Random House Webster's Collegiate Dictionary defines *"trample"* are, *"to domineer harshly; crush... To put out or extinguish by trampling."* Psalm 91:13 says, *"...and the serpent you shall trample underfoot."* How can you keep the devil under your feet on a daily basis?

2. Earlier, I wrote, "Have confidence in God and His plan.

You are a vital part of it. As a committed believer, you will be with the armies of heaven when Christ returns (Revelation 19:7-14)." How does knowing about God's ultimate victory help you to approach the battles you face in your present circumstances?

Paraphrase of the Second Section of Psalm 91
He Shall Give His Angels Charge Over You.

Verses 9-13

"The LORD, who is above all, reigns in sovereign majesty. Because you have chosen to make Him your abiding place (as I have), no intent to harm you shall be allowed to approach the place in which you dwell. {10} No evil that seeks a quarrel with you, in order to hurt you, will have the freedom to do so. God will protect you.

{11} These angels, on assignment from "God Most High," will take a "hands-on-approach" to what He has commanded them to do. {12} They will be your supporting and covering angelic defenders, upholding you, as God, Himself would. Their faithful actions will keep you from stumbling into or against whatever is placed before you to harm you. It will be as if the Lord Jesus Christ is stepping between you and your enemies, circumstances or trouble.

{13} You shall stomp and trample underfoot whatever evils endanger you. You shall walk safely beyond the threats of Satan, who is that dragon of old, the devil. You shall see the efforts of who or whatever desires to devour you (including all the schemes of the devil) become your stepping stones to victory - because God is with you and His angels have charge over you."

Part Three: The Divine Voice of Assurance
Verses 14-16

TEN

Your Love, His Name

Psalm 91:14

"Because he has set his love upon Me, therefore I will deliver him; I will set him on high, because he has known My name."

Up until this point, the voice in the psalm was the voice of humanity, in which the psalmist recited divinely inspired thoughts from his heart. However, in Verse 14, the psalmist put on the prophetic mantle. His writing recorded the voice of God, the *"Most High,"* Himself. Therefore, I have titled this Third Section of the psalm, "The Divine Voice of Assurance." It was no longer a second-person report of what God would do through His angels. It became a first-person guarantee from God, declared in His own voice. As you read the remainder of the psalm, you will notice the repeated use of the first-person personal pronoun, as God assures the reader that, *"I will..."* In this verse and the two that followed, God Himself declared His personal promise to those who dwell *"in the secret place."*

There can be no greater guarantee than when God has spoken directly to us. He did not say, *"Perhaps I will"* or *"I might if I feel like it."* No! God's words were full of loving care for us. He left no doubt that He would perform what

His Word promised. His promise was, is, and forever will remain, *"I will..."* Six times in the three final verses, His voice prophetically promises, *"I will."*

In Verse 14, God also spoke of how our love for Him influences Him. It moves Him to deliver His care on our behalf. As you have seen before in Psalm 91, the technique of cause and effect was used.

> Cause:
>
> *"BECAUSE he has set his love upon Me,"*
>
> Effect:
>
> *"...THEREFORE I will deliver him,"*
>
> Cause restated:
>
> *"...BECAUSE he has known My name."*
>
> Effect restated:
>
> *"I WILL set him on high,"*

Though at first it may seem so, Verse 14 is not a statement of pure grace. It is a direct response by the Almighty to our words, actions and hearts. As we have seen, the particular deliverance God guaranteed us in Psalm 91 is conditional on two complimentary responses. It requires your agreement and participation. You first must love Him; and, second, have an intimate knowledge of His name. The first condition speaks of an inward emotion that is outwardly demonstrated. The second condition is the result of a choice you make to become intimate with what the Bible calls *"a name above every name."* Knowing His name carries, within it, immeasurable value. It becomes our invitation to *"dwell"* with Him. Others, who do not know His name, will have no entry. The Hebrew word, translated into English as, *"name"* is *"yada."*[27] It speaks of the value of a relationship, not only with *"the Most High God,"* but also with His name. Its meaning can be paraphrased in this way: *"To have certain and respectful knowledge of something or someone."* It can also mean to know someone as a *"familiar friend"* or *"kinsman."*[28] Knowledge of the name of the Lord, and all it carries within it, brings about a God-directed, positive result - safety and security. Isn't it amazing that we have the privilege of being granted intimacy with this highest of names?

Understanding the incredible gift of intimately knowing the Lord's name brings us to the great doctrinal statement of Philippians, Chapter 2.

Philippians 2:5-11

"Let this mind be in you which was also in Christ Jesus, {6} who, being in the form of God, did not consider it robbery to be equal with God, {7} but made Himself of no reputation, taking the form of a bondservant, and coming in the likeness of men. {8} And being found in appearance as a man, He humbled Himself and became obedient to the point of death, even the death of the cross. {9} Therefore God also has highly exalted Him and given Him the name which is above every name, {10} that at the name of Jesus every knee should

---

[27] Strong's Number H8045.
[28] ibid.

> *bow, of those in heaven, and of those on earth, and of those under the earth, {11} and that every tongue should confess that Jesus Christ is Lord, to the glory of God the Father."*

These verses from Philippians reinforce what God says in Psalm 91:14. His promise is that whatever comes against you must bow its knee to the complete and final authority of the Lord Jesus Christ. God will move on behalf of the person who loves Jesus and knows His name. There can be no exceptions. Now, that is reassuring!

There is a story of a missionary in North Africa whose name is Frederick Nolan. It has been written about in many books and internet blogs. I have selected the version from "Tell Me a Story," which is an internet blog written by Mark Edge.[29]

> "Nolan was fleeing from his enemies during a time of persecution in North African. Vigilantly pursued by his foes, Nolan was running out of places to hide. Finally, bone-tired he came upon a small cave. Hiding inside, he expected his enemies to find him. Certain he was awaiting his death, he saw a spider begin to weave a web. Within minutes, the insect had woven an intricate web across the mouth of the cave. Shortly thereafter, his hunters arrived. At first, they suspected Nolan had entered the cave. Then, they considered how it would have been impossible for him to have entered without destroying the web.

---

[29] www.mark-edge-tellmeastory.blogspot.com/2010/09/god-and-spider-web.

So they left. Nolan escaped his potential captors. Later, contemplating his fate, he wrote, "Where God is, a spider's web is like a wall. Where God is not, a wall is like a spider's web.""

This story fits perfectly with God's promises in Psalm 91:14. Here is my paraphrase:

"Because My son Frederick Nolan set His love upon the Me and had intimate knowledge of My name, I intervened to deliver him from his pursuers. To demonstrate My sovereign will and power, I used the most fragile barrier there can be - a spider web, made from the finest silk of the spider. The web became a wall that set Frederick beyond the reach of his pursuers and their evil motives. They would not, and could not penetrate it to harm my beloved son, Frederick."

Things to Think About

1. Why do you think God interjected His voice into the final three verses of the psalm?
2. Can you explain how grace can sometimes be dependent on what we do, but at other times be sovereignly given?

ELEVEN

The Divine Voice of Assurance

Psalms 91:15

"He shall call upon Me, and I will answer him; I will be with him in trouble; I will deliver him and honor him."

God continued to elaborate on the process in which He would respond to the call for help from one of His children. The verse contains three separate messages, working together. Let's unpack them:

1. God responds to those who call upon Him.

   Generally speaking, we must be careful not to limit God's response to a requirement that we ask Him for help. Often He will move sovereignly. He may even intercede preemptively when we are still unaware of the threat. However, this particular promise of deliverance fits within the literary context of the entire psalm. God was being specific; and, His words showed that He takes the issue of our safety personally. At the end of the psalm, with His own voice, God has assured us of His presence and personal intervention, when we call upon Him. He will truly be with us and will be our refuge.

Psalm 50:15

"Call upon Me in the day of trouble; I will deliver you, and you shall glorify Me."

Jeremiah 29:11-12

"For I know the thoughts that I think toward you, says the LORD, thoughts of peace and not of evil, to give you a future and a hope. {12} Then you will call upon Me and go and pray to Me, and I will listen to you."

Joel 2:32a

"And it shall come to pass That whoever calls on the name of the LORD Shall be saved."

1 John 5:14-15

"Now this is the confidence that we have in Him, that if we as anything according to His will, He hears us. {15} And if we know that He hears us, whatever we ask, we know that we have the petitions that we have asked of Him."

Our confidence is in God, who is always faithful to hear and respond. Be sure you keep your heart turned to the will of God; and, watch Him perform His Word over you.

2. God voiced His promise that He would deliver us, as He provides close fellowship with us throughout our trouble, His heart would be touched with the hurts we experience. He would share what we go through; and, take us to the other side.

There are many assurances of God's intervention throughout both testaments. The Apostle Paul wrote to Timothy of how the Lord had been there to deliver him from *"the mouth of the lion"* (perhaps a metaphor); and, would deliver him from *"every evil work."* This was a testimony of God's awareness of Paul's difficulties and His faithfulness to answer Paul's prayers. We can claim this principle of divine intervention for ourselves. God will be there for us, as we trust, honor and serve Him. He will not be a casual observer.

2 Timothy 4:17-18

"But the Lord stood with me and strengthened me, so that the message might be preached fully through me, and that all the Gentiles might hear. And I was delivered out of the mouth of the lion. {18} And the Lord will deliver me from every evil work and preserve me for His heavenly kingdom. To Him be glory forever and ever. Amen"

On the cross, Jesus experienced every hurt that we may experience. He understands our trouble and pain. He will never abandon us. The Bible gives reference to our opportunity to join with Him in *"the fellowship of His suffering."* The Apostle Paul certainly experienced this fellowship on many occasions.

Philippians 3:10

"that I may know Him and the power of His resurrection, and the fellowship of His sufferings, being conformed to His death,"

Paul knew that our suffering could not match what Christ endured on the cross, or what the Father suffered in having to turn away in the midst of Jesus' passion. However, Paul's experiences taught him that when we suffer, we have the opportunity to remain tightly locked in an intimate, personal relationship with our Father God. He will never again turn His back. He will answer when we call upon Him. This is our eternal guarantee, backed by the blood of Jesus.

God's promise that He will be with us to deliver us may not happen in the way we want. Nevertheless, His promises are true. We can rely on His word that He will hear and deliver us into something far better than what we may be suffering at the moment. The Hebrew word used in Psalm 91:15 for *"deliver"* is *"chalats."*[30] This word has many flavors of meaning; but one that fit perfectly with God's intent of this verse is to *"withdraw"* us from the threat. Another meaning is to *"arm"* us. This means that God often chooses to forego direct intervention in favor of equipping us to battle our way out of the situation. God will provide any number of ways for this to happen. All of them will have spiritual foundations that will facilitate natural solutions.

Ephesians 6:10-14

"Finally, my brethren, be strong in the Lord and in the power of His might. {11} Put on the whole armor of God, that you may be able to stand against the wiles of the devil. {12} For we do not

---

[30] Strong's Number H2502.

wrestle against flesh and blood, but against principalities, against powers, against the rulers of the darkness of this age, against spiritual hosts of wickedness in the heavenly places. {13} Therefore take up the whole armor of God, that you may be able to withstand in the evil day, and having done all, to stand. {14} Stand therefore, having girded your waist with truth, having put on the breastplate of righteousness,"

2 Corinthians 10:3-7

"For though we walk in the flesh, we do not war according to the flesh. {4} For the weapons of our warfare are not carnal but mighty in God for pulling down strongholds, {5} casting down arguments and every high thing that exalts itself against the knowledge of God, bringing every thought into captivity to the obedience of Christ, {6} and being ready to punish all disobedience when your obedience is fulfilled. {7} Do you look at things according to the outward appearance? If anyone is convinced in himself that he is Christ's, let him again consider this in himself, that just as he is Christ's, even so we are Christ's."

Paul knew that the battleground might go beyond the physical realm. It may be a completely spiritual battle. It may be an emotional battle. (In some cases, it may be a battle in all three realms.) Following are examples of how the Holy Spirit illustrated this through Paul's epistles.

Regardless of how the battle manifests, and however God chooses to provide deliverance to us, we will be *"more than conquerors"* because of His promise to intervene. We can trust this promise because it has His perfect love and unending faithfulness as its foundation.

Romans 8:35-39

"Who shall separate us from the love of Christ? Shall tribulation, or distress, or persecution, or famine, or nakedness, or peril, or sword? {36} As it is written: "For Your sake we are killed all day long; We are accounted as sheep for the slaughter." {37} Yet in all these things we are more than conquerors through Him who loved us. {38} For I am persuaded that neither death nor life, nor angels nor principalities nor powers, nor things present nor things to come, {39} nor height nor depth, nor any other created thing, shall be able to separate us from the love of God which is in Christ Jesus our Lord."

3. God completed His promises of Psalm 91:15 by saying, *"I will honor him."* We should not overlook the significance of our all-powerful, majestic, *Most High God"* honoring us because we *"set our love upon Him."* His promise that He will honor us, even in light of our sinful, imperfect lives, is an unexpected and undeserved gift. It is a demonstration of grace that invites considerable reflection.

Why would God, who cannot stand being in the presence of sin, honor us who remain stained with the curse of original sin that came to us from Adam? We are, after all, certainly less than holy. We all find ourselves, in some small way, dishonoring Him on a daily basis. The answer is threefold:

First, Christ has redeemed us from what the Apostle Paul called, *"the law of sin and death."*[31] Christ did this through His own death on the cross. Because of the Son's obedience, the Father now honors us. We are justified by our faith in Christ. Our debt for dishonoring God, as a hereditary issue and a current one, has been paid in full. The rebellious, sinful nature we inherited from the *"first Adam"* has been denied its power, through the atoning work of the *"last Adam,"* the Lord Jesus Christ.

1 Corinthians 15:45

"And so it is written, "The first man Adam became a living being. The last Adam became a life-giving spirit.""

Romans 8:1-2

"There is therefore now no condemnation to those who are in Christ Jesus, who do not walk according to the flesh, but according to the Spirit. {2} For the law of the Spirit of life in Christ Jesus has made me free from the law of sin and death."

Second, when you accepted Christ as Lord and Savior, you gained a new spiritual nature that holds within it, the potential to grow continually more like Jesus. God will

---

[31] Romans 8:1-2.

always honor your efforts to do so. You can act like, think like, speak like and love like Jesus. This can increase progressively more, every day. You can grow into a place where you consistently please the Father, and where it is His good pleasure to hear, join with, deliver and honor you because of what He finds in your heart.

Third, the Father's loving nature is so divinely perfect and strong, that He cannot help but honor you with His love. Even when you were dead spiritually, buried in your sins, He still loved you. Now, as you enjoy rising from the ashes of the past, and living under His glory in the present, He rejoices over you. When you cling to Him, He responds, as your *"Abba."* His is the completely dependable divine voice of assurance. Pause for a moment and listen. Let Him speak to you. He will assure you that your loving intentions toward Him have put you in His *"secret place."*

Things to Think About

1. What would be your definition of *"the fellowship of His suffering."* How would this apply to Christian life today?

2. Why would the Apostle Paul be so concerned with describing our spiritual foundations as *"weapons"*? What other Scriptures validate this concern?

3. Using simple terms of every-day speech, how would you define living *"according to the Spirit"*?

TWELVE

Satisfaction, Now and Forever

Psalms 91:16

"With long life I will satisfy him, And show him My salvation."

In His perfect wisdom, God ends the psalm with two final promises. The first has to do with our earthly, carnal, temporal lives. It appeals to our natural desire to live. The second has to do with our eternal existence and appeals to our understanding of who we are in Christ. Only the second can bring us consistent peace. Even in the midst of the emotional bounces we all experience, we can know that God has promised us eternity with Him. He is always thinking of us. Therefore, we can trust in Him to keep us in *"perfect peace."*

Isaiah 26:3-4

"You will keep him in perfect peace, Whose mind is stayed on You, Because he trusts in You. {4} Trust in the LORD forever, For in YAH, the LORD, is everlasting strength."

When God promised us long life, He was not saying He would prolong our earthly days beyond our time. He was saying that He would intervene (as is consistent with the entire psalm) to keep anything or anyone from cutting short our days. We would fulfill all the days we have been given by God. *"Perfect peace"* will come from knowing that our earthly days are in the Lord's hands, not anyone else's. The full number of our days and the eternity beyond them is God's personally stated guarantee. At the end of our earthly days, as we go beyond death to the glorious moment when we will begin to live forever with Christ, we can be satisfied. We will have run our race and the prize will be ours.

John the Revelator's Testimony

Revelation 21:3-4

"And I heard a loud voice from heaven saying, "Behold, the tabernacle of God is with men, and He will dwell with them, and they shall be His people. God Himself will be with them and be their God. {4} And God will wipe away every tear from their eyes; there shall be no more death, nor sorrow, nor crying. There shall be no more pain, for the former things have passed away.""

Revelation 21:3-4 (My paraphrase)

"I will reveal to my faithful servant (with full clarity and in the brightness of My presence) what the fullness of salvation really brings to him or her. There shall be no more tears, sorrow, crying or pain. Death will never again be an issue. What will make this so special is that I will personally wipe the tears away with My gentle hand of loving care."

Things to Think About

1. Something perfect may be defined as entirely without flaws or defects. When Isaiah 26:3 speaks of *"perfect peace,"* it describes an emotionally restful state of mind that flawlessly reacts to whatever situation might be unsettling. Why does God's guarantee in the final verse of Psalm 91 have the potential to take you to *"perfect peace"*?

2. What is the prize awaiting you when your race is finished? (Take your answer beyond the obvious - that we have eternity with Christ.)

Paraphrase of the Third Section of Psalm 91
The Divine Voice of Assurance

Verses 14-16

"Because you set your love upon the Me; and, because you have intimate knowledge of My name, I will intervene to deliver you from your pursuers. To demonstrate My sovereign will and power, I will use any means I choose. It may be to erect a supernatural barrier to set you beyond the reach of your pursuers and their evil motives. It may be to send angels to act on My behalf. It may be that I will intervene personally, by the power of My Spirit. However I choose to bring deliverance, you may be sure that nothing will harm you. {15} Be assured that when you call upon Me, I will not hesitate an instant to answer you. I will walk

through your trouble with you. I will carry him all the way through it. I will strike a powerful blow against whatever is against you. You will find yourself free of it. All this I will do, as My sovereign act of honoring you, as you have honored Me. It will be nothing less than an act of covenant commitment on My behalf. {16} I will reveal to you, My faithful servant (with full clarity) in the brightness of My presence, what the fullness of salvation really brings to you. There shall be no more tears, sorrow, crying or pain. Death will never again be an issue. What will make this so special is that I will personally wipe the tears away with My gentle hand of loving care."

REFLECTIONS

Psalm 91: A Gift that Keeps Giving

Regardless of how much you analyze or unwrap its meanings, Psalm 91 always has more to say to you. Indeed, it is a gift that keeps giving. It is God's assurance that His intervention will always fit the need and defeat the threat. There are no exceptions. When God moves into a situation, everything involved must bow its knee and acknowledge that Jesus Christ is Lord. As you read earlier, the Apostle Paul defined this process perfectly in Philippians, Chapter 2. He wrote of Christ the King, who is Creator, Deliverer and Sovereign Judge. Paul described Jesus' sacrifice, and how the mention of His name affected whomever or whatever evil faces the Lord's intervention. It is well worth repeating Paul's words as we come to the conclusion of the book:

Philippians 2:8-11

"And being found in appearance as a man, He humbled Himself and became obedient to the point of death, even the death of the cross. {9} Therefore God also has highly exalted Him and given Him the name which is above every name, {10} that at the name of Jesus every knee should bow, of those in heaven, and of those on earth, and of those under the earth, {11} and that every

tongue should confess that Jesus Christ is Lord, to the glory of God the Father."

Psalm 91 has assured us that there will be no confusion or guessing when God moves into your circumstances to deliver you. You will know with certainty that God will move on your behalf. Not only will you have the indisputable guarantee of His Word, from His own voice in Psalm 91:14-16, but He will put His personal signature on whatever He does. This is the final, indisputable stamp of His authority. It carries the full authorization of heaven. It has been signed with the blood of Christ.

Romans 8:31-32

"What then shall we say to these things? If God is for us, who can be against us? {32} He who did not spare His own Son, but delivered Him up for us all, how shall He not with Him also freely give us all things?"

God has guaranteed that He will do His part. Nevertheless, this remains conditional. Will you do your part? Will you love, trust and obey Him? When these three conditions are fulfilled, you will never have to go it alone.

At the beginning of the book, you read of a picture that formed in my mind of a tree house that had been lovingly built by a father for his child. It was a safe place where time would be spent letting all kinds of wonderful imaginations, hopes and dreams run free. One of the best things about it is that the father and child, a big dad and little kid, would spend time together in a place made just for them.

"The secret place" is always accessible to the child of God who seeks a close, intimate relationship with the Father. Let it beckon you to enter. Jesus paid your price of admission. Will you allow Him to draw you into the depths of a relationship with Him you have not yet experienced. It will be worth every moment. He will be with you. He will be for you. He will perform His Word over you. Then, you can be just like " A Kid in God's Tree House."

Dr. Bob Abramson

Complete Paraphrase of Psalm 91

"Whoever quietly and constantly remains at rest in that hidden place in God, will be comfortably at home, secure in his relationship with the One who is above all others, and has the power to guarantee security, safety and peace. {2} I will say of the LORD (I will not keep silent) He is my protection and a wall between me and whatever wants to harm me.

{3} Surely, without any doubt or hesitation, the LORD will prevent you from being trapped and destroyed like a bird in the cage of a fowler. He will even stop the perils and wicked attacks of deadly, life-threatening diseases or plagues. This holds true for unusual and perverse calamities.

{4} Caring for you as an eagle cares for its young, God will place you under the unfailing wings of His power and love. You will be secure beyond the reach of any evil intent. This means when you place yourself under the unfailing covering of God's protection and refuge, you can trust Him to keep you safe and secure, as He brings life to your hopes, dreams and visions.

{5} Have no fear of the unknown that may come out of the darkness and uncertainties of a night without any light to see it coming. God will protect you from the sudden, unseen dangers of demonic spiritual activities. {6} He will also stop the random contagion and disease that picks its victim with deliberate malice and intent. Even

when it attempts an "in your face" assault on your faith, God will be there to move into the assault on your behalf.

{7} Many may fall (even multitudes), as they become victim to the things they fear. However, in spite of what seems to leave you a lone, insignificant person among many, God guarantees that when you position yourself under the shadow of His wing, and place your trust completely in Him, He will keep the trouble at a distance from you. {8} Believe and trust in the LORD. You will be an eyewitness to the destruction of what has tried to destroy you.

{9} The LORD, who is above all, reigns in sovereign majesty. Because you have chosen to make Him your abiding place (as I have), no intent to harm you shall be allowed to approach the place in which you dwell. {10} No evil that seeks a quarrel with you, in order to hurt you, will have the freedom to do so. God will protect you. {11} The angels, on assignment from "God Most High," will take a "hands-on-approach" to what He has commanded them to do. {12} They will be your supporting and covering angelic defenders, upholding you, as God, Himself would. Their faithful actions will keep you from stumbling into or against whatever is placed before you to harm you. It will be as if the Lord Jesus Christ is stepping between you and your enemies, circumstances or trouble. {13} You shall stomp

and trample underfoot whatever evils endanger you. You shall walk safely beyond the threats of Satan, who is that dragon of old, the devil. You shall see the efforts of who or whatever desires to devour you (including all the schemes of the devil) become your stepping-stones to victory - because God is with you and His angels have charge over you.

{14} Because you set your love upon the Me; and, because you have intimate knowledge of My name, I will intervene to deliver you from your pursuers. To demonstrate My sovereign will and power, I will use any means I choose. It may be to erect a supernatural barrier to set you beyond the reach of your pursuers and their evil motives. It may be to send angels to act on My behalf. It may be that I will intervene personally, by the power of My Spirit. However I choose to bring deliverance, you may be sure that nothing will harm you. {15} Be assured that when you call upon Me, I will not hesitate an instant to answer you. I will walk through your trouble with you. I will carry him all the way through it. I will strike a powerful blow against whatever is against you. You will find yourself free of it. All this I will do, as My sovereign act of honoring you, as you have honored Me. It will be nothing less than an act of covenant commitment on My behalf. {16} I will reveal to you, My faithful servant (with full clarity) in the brightness of My presence, what the fullness of salvation really brings to you. There

shall be no more tears, sorrow, crying or pain. Death will never again be an issue. What will make this so special is that I will personally wipe the tears away with My gentle hand of loving care."

Let the words of Psalm Ninety-One and the meditations of your heart flow together in harmony, as you serve our God Most High.

He is forever faithful. Amen.

Dr. Bob Abramson
(Just a Kid in God's Tree House)

APPENDIX

Additional Scriptures and Notes
"the secret place"

In addition to Psalm 91, at least ten other Scriptures in the New King James Version mention *"the secret place."* Four are of particular relevance. Each provides support to the theme that you have somewhere to go, and someone to whom you can turn in time of trouble or uncertainty. All speak of God's intervention. Of the four I have referenced below, three are in the Psalms and the fourth is in the Book of Matthew. (This fourth example recorded Jesus' own words of instruction regarding prayer, which ought to be our first response to trouble.)

Psalms 27:5

"For in the time of trouble He shall hide me in His pavilion; In the secret place of His tabernacle He shall hide me; He shall set me high upon a rock."

This verse speaks of God's provision of a safe place, that is hidden from the view of your enemies or trouble. It is unique and special because it is *"in the secret place of His tabernacle."* This simply means it is in the holy place where God has chosen to abide… and you have entrance to it. The psalmist spoke metaphorically, when he wrote, *"He shall set me high upon a rock."* The reference was to the child of God being positioned above and beyond the reach of the trouble.

Psalms 31:19-20

"Oh, how great is Your goodness, Which You have laid up for those who fear You, Which You have prepared for those who trust in You In the presence of the sons of men! {20} You shall hide them in the secret place of Your presence From the plots of man; You shall keep them secretly in a pavilion From the strife of tongues."

In these two verses, the psalmist emphasized the goodness of God (and all the protection it contains), which is stored up for those who honor and revere Him. The emphasis here is to trust Him with everything you have, knowing that when the plots of those who have gathered against you are voiced, God will hear their words. His response will be to protect you, as He hides you *"secretly in a pavilion."* The plans they have voiced will come to nothing, because God will be there to keep you safe.

Psalms 81:7

"You called in trouble, and I delivered you; I answered you in the secret place of thunder; I tested you at the waters of Meribah. Selah"

Here, as in Psalm 91:14-16, the speaker is God. It is a reminder of God's deliverance of Israel, even when they tried to test Him with their hardened hearts. God showed His faithfulness then and will show it now. Below, is the historical reference to this event in the Book of Numbers. It happened in the desert *"at the waters of Meribah."*

Numbers 20:10-13

"And Moses and Aaron gathered the assembly together before the rock; and he said to them, "Hear now, you rebels! Must we bring water for you out of this rock?" {11} Then Moses lifted his hand and struck the rock twice with his rod; and water came out abundantly, and the congregation and their animals drank. {12} Then the LORD spoke to Moses and Aaron, "Because you did not believe Me, to hallow Me in the eyes of the children of Israel, therefore you shall not bring this assembly into the land which I have given them." {13} This was the water of Meribah, because the children of Israel contended with the LORD, and He was hallowed among them."

Numbers 20:13 (NLT)

"This place was known as the waters of Meribah, because it was where the people of Israel argued with the LORD, and where he demonstrated his holiness among them."

The New Living Translation of Numbers 20:13 illustrates the incredible grace of God. The Bible tells us that, at Meribah, *"he demonstrated his holiness among them."* We correctly can conclude that the holiness or perfection of God is absolute. He will honor His word with signs following. At

Meribah, the water gushed from the rock to provide for the Israelites, in spite of their rebellion. (Some of the ways of God are difficult to understand, because He is sovereign and does not react as we would.)

Matthew 6:6

"But you, when you pray, go into your room, and when you have shut your door, pray to your Father who is in the secret place; and your Father who sees in secret will reward you openly."

In Matthew 6:6, we have an inspired word of confirmation that *"the secret place"* is as timeless as God. Here, Jesus confirmed that when you pray, even at this very moment, your heavenly Father will be found in His *"secret place."* Jesus' own words provide New Testament confirmation of Psalm 91 and its continuing message.

An appropriate conclusion to this appendix would be the Message Bible's translation of Romans 8:31-39. These Scriptures truly complete Paul's thoughts and describe what I have written in the pages of this book.

Romans 8:31-39 (MSG)

"So, what do you think? With God on our side like this, how can we lose? If God didn't hesitate to put everything on the line for us, embracing our condition and exposing himself to the worst by sending his own Son, is there anything else he wouldn't gladly and freely do for us? And who would dare tangle with God by messing with one

of God's chosen? Who would dare even to point a finger? The One who died for us - who was raised to life for us! - is in the presence of God at this very moment sticking up for us. Do you think anyone is going to be able to drive a wedge between us and Christ's love for us? There is no way! Not trouble, not hard times, not hatred, not hunger, not homelessness, not bullying threats, not backstabbing, not even the worst sins listed in Scripture:

They kill us in cold blood because they hate you. We're sitting ducks; they pick us off one by one.

None of this fazes us because Jesus loves us. I'm absolutely convinced that nothing - nothing living or dead, angelic or demonic, today or tomorrow, high or low, thinkable or unthinkable - absolutely nothing can get between us and God's love because of the way that Jesus our Master has embraced us."

Well, we are finished. I will leave you to answer this question from Romans 8:31 of the Message Bible: *"So, what do you think? With God on our side like this, how can we lose?*

Selah

About Dr. Bob Abramson

Dr. Abramson has extensive experience as a cross-cultural mentor and educator of those in the five-fold ministry. He and his wife Nancy have pastored international churches in New York City and the Fiji Islands in the South Pacific. He established or taught in Bible schools and ministry training centers in New Zealand, Fiji, Taiwan, Hong Kong, Malaysia, Europe and the United States. He provides free resources worldwide through his website, "Mentoring Ministry" (www.mentoringministry.com).

Dr. Abramson earned a Doctor of Ministry from Erskine Theological Seminary, a Masters in Religion from Liberty University and a Bachelor of Arts in the Bible with a minor in Systematic Theology from Southeastern University. He and his wife Nancy live in Lake Worth, Florida. They have five grown children and seven grandchildren.

Contact Dr. Abramson, at www.mentoringministry.com
or write him at Dr.Bob@mentoringministry.com

Dr. Abramson is the author of these books.

- "Just a Little Bit More - The Heart of a Mentor"
  (Book and Workbook)
- "The Leadership Puzzle"
  (Two Workbooks and The Facilitator's Manual)
- "Growing Together, Marriage Enrichment for Every Culture."
  (Book and Workbook)
- "Reflections - Spiritual Food for Thought," Volumes One-Three"
  (This is a series of devotional journals.)
- "Stepping Stones" (100 illustrated, full color sermon outlines)
- "Moral Manhood - Swimming with the Sharks"
- "Focus on the Father - The Lord's Prayers"
- "God's Kind of Love - A Journey of the Heart"
- "The Fullness of the Holy Spirit In You, For You and With You"

Made in the USA
Charleston, SC
04 March 2017